I KNOW A
ROTTEN PLACE

Bryan Breed

John Clare Books
London

First published 1975 by Arlington Books Ltd.

Reprinted 1980

This edition 1995 by John Clare Books,

© Bryan Breed

ISBN 0-906549-59-0

Printed and bound by Short Run Press Ltd., Exeter

Introduction

During the Second World War thousands of children were sent away from the bombing to earn the title of evacuees. This book tries to tell what happened to two of them. If at times I have seen the people who took us into their homes with a jaundiced eye, I hope they will forgive me. It is very difficult for an uprooted child to be anything but subjective. Now I can only marvel at the kind souls who bravely put up with our antics, our rudeness, and our longing to be home again. Their kindness in the face of the long odds against them of ever winning our affection was considerable They saw it in terms of their duty, of doing their bit during a long war, but only now can I realise what it must have cost them and what influence they must have had on our futures.

Chapter I

We had been with our mother and father in a warm unawareness of the world in our tenement flat near the Thames in Stepney, when, suddenly, they had said we would have to go away. It was for our own good. It would stop us from getting hurt when the bombs came. What was a bomb anyway? And as we marched two-by-two, five and six years old respectively, gas-mask cases over our macs, waving to our Mum, who stood by the school railings with the others, a handkerchief in every hand, nothing, not even these bombs, could hurt as much as that.

I did not know then that it was 1939, or anything much about Germans and aeroplanes. Aeroplanes had been moths, a sleepy, droning background noise to a summer day's outing in Essex or at Hadleigh Woods, playing on Dad's back wearing a knitted woollen bathing costume with somebody else's name embroidered on it.

It was Mum who just said we would have to go away. She could not come with us, and nor could Dad. Our teacher, Mrs Naylor, had been talking about it for ages. We did not really know what she was on about. She had started at about the same time as the black gas-masks, with the long-nosed, fly-catcher bottoms, and the cellophane strip that allowed you a look at the outside world. The tight band went over your ears and when your head was inside it smelt terrible. I did not like putting it on. I felt as if I was choking.

But I just had to struggle into it with all the others in our class because some horrible men called Germans were going to come over in aeroplanes and drop some stuff from the sky. Some of it was made of mustard and it would burn us and make us ill if we breathed it. Mrs Naylor said the heavy thing with the holes in the bottom would stop this. The mustard would not get through these holes, she said, even though we breathed. I knew mustard burnt my tongue so I pulled the smelly thing over my head and breathed. Mrs Naylor would make a funny noise, wailing away, pretending to be an air-raid siren, and we all had to find our cardboard cases and put on the rubber masks.

Sometimes she would wail when we were in the middle of eating our thick soup at dinner time. I got the soup for David and me. Two pennies were thrust into my hand by my mother at the iron school gates. I exchanged these in the classroom for two coloured plastic discs like you played tiddly-winks with. I never did think this was much of a bargain at the time, but it always did the trick when you gave them to the woman in the little hall with red and blue window panes. It was a church school, St Paul's, Wellclose Square. It always smelt like burning coffee, the school.

There was a factory right alongside the school which sent up smoke signals by roasting coffee. You could see and smell them as you dashed around the playground, with its white dusty ground and the tree every few yards. I was always running into the thick trunks and getting awarded a piece of sticky plaster over an eye or my nose which all the other kids admired. I didn't mind the trees at all, because in the summer there were greeny-yellow things crawling up the trunks, and sometimes on the lower leaves you could find a red beetle with black spots. The big boys showed me what to do. You picked up the leaf and blew on the red things, and said softly:

"Fly away ladybird, fly away home. Your house is on fire and your children are home."

If you blew hard enough the red shell parted and wings appeared and away it went. But sometimes the obstinate thing would not

believe that her house was on fire and refused to move from her place
in the sun. Then the big boys would give it a gentle tap, often with
quite fatal results, and they would arrange a funeral service and put
what was left in a matchbox under a stone.

It was past these same trees and through the burning coffee that we
marched along in twos that first day, all wearing mackintoshes, belted
tightly in the middle, each clutching a brown paper bag of food a
teacher had pushed into our hands. We were going away from the
war, they had said.

Soon, said the Spanish lady along the landing from us in Peabody's,
the block of flats where we lived, Hitler would be dropping bombs on
us all, then he would try to swim across the Channel and invade us. If
the soldiers did not stop him, he would put most of us into sausage
machines to feed his troops. She knew, Mum said. She had just run
away from Spain, like we were having to run away, and she had seen
it happen there.

We went round Wellclose Square, the mums keeping pace for a
bit, waving, some trying to look cheerful, some not managing it.
When we reached Cable Street the pavement was too narrow and the
mothers started to drop away. We were going down a tube, Mrs
Naylor had said, then into a big green train that would hold all of us.
The long caterpillar of a school crawled up Watney Street. Some of
the kids were already crying because they thought they might never
see their mums again.

"It won't be for long," Mum had said.

But how long was long, and what if Hitler swam the Channel
before we got back? One of the teachers showed a man a piece of
paper and the caterpillar began to disappear into Shadwell underground station. Watney Street was where the market was and a few
of the stallholders and shoppers stopped to watch us go.

"Ah, love 'em," said one woman.

"Poor little sods," someone else said. "Still, it's better than them
being blown up by one of them bleeding bombs."

"We change at Whitechapel," was all that Mrs Naylor said,
"remember that."

At Victoria they packed us all into the big green train. Somebody kept on saying we were going to somewhere called Eastbourne and that it would be nice because it was the seaside. I didn't care where it was. I didn't want to be there. At that moment there was only one place I wanted to be and that was in the plain distempered walls of home. I kept on wondering what would happen when we got there, and finally I got near enough to Mrs Naylor to ask. We'd get new parents, who would look after us until the war was over, but that would not be for long. I didn't want new parents, and I knew David didn't as he sat down next to me on the green train.

The train kept stopping and then starting. It was because it was an evacuee train, Mrs Naylor said, and they had to fit them in between all the normal ones. When it had stopped nowhere for the fourth time, somebody popped her head round the door and said we could start on our dinners: cheese sandwiches and a big round biscuit like the ones we had thrust into our hands when we had to wait outside the pub on the odd occasion my parents went for a drink.

We were all finished and there were crumbs all over the floor when the train stopped at Eastbourne station. We were lined up on the platform, and then off we went again, David grasping my hand. As we went past, people stopped and stared and a few of them laughed.

Eventually we went up a hill and turned into the gates of a school. It was a posh one, with a tar playground, and no dust or thick trees like Wellcose Square. Inside there were lots of green ladies, with round hats, who fussed and made noises over us.

"So good of the W.V.S. to help," said Mrs Naylor, who seemed to sound posher all of a sudden.

After the clucking was over they sat us down to drink milk and to count us. Then this tall woman started to call out names in a deep voice. We were some of the first to be called.

"David and Bryan Reed."

I knew they meant us because people always forget to put the B in front. I grabbed hold of David's mac sleeve and pulled him forward. We were pushed into a group. Mrs Naylor was in the centre, rubbing the hair of those who had started to cry again. There were a lot with snotty noses and I rubbed my sleeve across mine and David's to make sure ours were clear of candlesticks.

"That lot's for just up the road," said the woman with the deep voice and the big board that had all our names on it. "You'd better round them up and get moving or you won't get them billeted until after it's dark."

Nobody seemed ready to move very quickly. Each stage had given its own touch of security. Nobody had wanted to leave the train, despite the fact that the carriages were beginning to smell a bit. We'd all started singing after a while. It was a bit like the country outings from the East End Mission, though, of course, you didn't need your gas-mask then. The school, too, had put off the final trip into the unknown, but now it had come at last. Everybody was tired and very quiet.

The gardens in front of the houses looked funny. Little handkerchiefs of grass or flowers, which nobody ever touched. Different to the square.

"Mum, can we go and play in the square? We won't go out through the front gate or knock on Mrs Lear's door."

The square was our concrete, communal playground where all the kids ran around and shouted and nobody worried, not even the people who lived on the ground floor, because that was the way it had always been. Mrs Lear was the fat German lady who lived up the landing from us, and who had two daughters who wore thick glasses and already had moustaches. Nobody liked her and the kids realised this and tormented her by knocking on her door and making her haul herself to it before disappearing round the corner and laughing.

The square was a lovely place, a cowboy and Indian round every block corner, a race track for the leg-aching little red motor-cars which made us the terror of every old lady, and caused them to swing their shopping bags at us.

There did not seem to be any Red Indians behind these hedges, and what would the bloke in the big house do if you churned up his grass with your tin car wheels. But then there had not been room to bring the battered toy motor-cars with us.

Dave and I were the first to go, the first pair to be parted from the herd of sad and dismal-looking evacuees. They all stopped outside a big house, with white walls and thick black criss-cross stripes, and they stared at it. The lady in green steered David and me in by the back of our heads.

"I'll get these two inside, then I'll catch you down the road. The next stop isn't until Hunter's End right down there on the left."

As we went through the gate I looked back, feeling scared. The rest of them were staring over their shoulders as they walked. I took hold of David's hand and pretended to be quite brave, and, in a way, I felt proud at being the first to face . . . what?

The green lady hurried us along the path down the side of the house. I wondered why we did not use the big black wooden door at the front. Perhaps there was a big trap door behind it to keep people from getting in, especially people like Germans when Hitler swam the Channel. The man whose house it was just pulled a toilet chain and down you went hardly ever to be seen again.

When the green lady rapped in a military fashion on the door at the back this woman came out. She just said:

"Oh."

Then she stood and looked at us for ages, eyes travelling over parted macs and down the new shirts and trousers, too long, that Mum had bought us specially. We didn't know what to do or what to say, so we just looked back at her. She wasn't old, but she wasn't young either. She looked as if she was worried about something. The green lady finished it by pushing us forward and a piece of paper into her hand.

"These are your evacuees. Must fly down to Hunter's End before the others get there."

The old-young lady didn't seem too sure about us or what to do with us. She didn't seem to want to touch us, and backed into the room behind waving us to follow her. When we could see round her, there were two of the oldest people I had ever seen. The old lady was examining us over the top of thick glasses, the man over the top of a newspaper. There was something queer about him. He had a glass stuck in one eye. None of them smiled. They seemed as stunned as the one who had come to the door.

"This is Mother and Father," said the old-young lady at last. "We'll be looking after you."

The daughter started messing around, taking off our macs, holding them out at the top of two fingers and examining them as if she was looking for something. The other two said nothing, just looking.

"Sit down at the table," said the daughter. She brought a white cloth and spread it over the table. What was that for? The table looked clean enough. Then she brought a milk and a sandwich.

"Not more bloody sandwiches," David blurted out before I could kick him under the table.

The daughter dropped the knives she was carrying and went red. For the first time the fat old woman spoke:

"What was that he said? Nobody says words like that in Eastbourne. We wash out the mouths of little boys who say words like that with soap and water. Father isn't used to words like that, and I don't expect Gladys has ever heard the likes of it before . . ."

"They told me you'd had a meal on the train," broke in Gladys quickly, as if she was trying to change the subject. "But anyway you'd better not have too much before you go to bed."

Bed. Already? It was only about six o'clock and at home we always went to bed later than that, and I remember that once when Dad was working nights Mum had allowed us to stay up until something called midnight. How long, I'd kept asking. When the two hands come together straight, Mum had said. Now it was only six and I felt as if they wanted to get rid of us, perhaps so that they could talk about us. Gladys was looking at her mother. She did not seem to do anything without looking at her mother.

"After that train journey they had better have a bath."

"I should think so, too," said Mother with a funny look on her face.

David's moon face was going from one to another, not knowing what to make of it all. I knew what he was thinking though. A bath? Tonight? We'd only had one the night before, the big tin bath put down on the mat in front of the old black cooking range that Mum seemed to polish for nothing. There was no fire here and I wondered where they kept the tin bath.

In Peabody's the tin bath was kept in the wash-house everybody used in the middle of the landing, and we bathed in that most of the time, but occasionally there was a visit to the public baths in Betts Street. That was a marvellous place because it was really only for grown-ups, but we had been smuggled in once or twice. When you got into the bath-house it was all warm and steamy and the grown-ups sat along the side on a bench clutching a towel marked Stepney Borough Council in red letters and a little bar of soap. Loan of the towel, soap and water cost a penny, and there was often a bit of soap left you could bring home with you.

The attendant let in the water with a special key from the outside of each little cubicle. Some people took liberties with the hot water and could not be trusted to let in their own.

It was a happy place. They would all be singing as they scrubbed themselves, and through it all the attendant was in great demand.

"More 'ot number four, Jack."

"More cold, Jack."

Sometimes Jack would grumble because somebody asked for hot, then immediately for cold.

"What you want, Jack . . . you want I should cook my balls off just to save you the trouble of walking a few steps?"

Sometimes there would be jokes. Somebody would call out for more hot water in number fifteen when they themselves were in number nine, and number fifteen would yell and shout at Jack out of shock.

"You'd better do it, Mum," said Gladys going red again.

"They're only children," Mum said scornfully. "They won't mind."

Gladys did not seem to know much about little boys, and she still kept blushing.

"Oh, all right, all right," said Mum. "Because it's the first time I'll help, but don't expect it every time."

Then, turning to us: "Come on you two. It's upstairs."

Upstairs? That was funny for a start. We'd never lived anywhere that had an upstairs. In Peabody's upstairs were the people who lived over the top of you, and downstairs was the people underneath.

Sometimes, if you bounced a ball or jumped on and off the bed, the people downstairs would bang on the ceiling with a broom. Just to keep up the custom Mum would get out her broom and bang upstairs when they were having a row which the whole block could hear. It meant they did not talk for a few days, but everybody got over it in the end, because you were all so close together you had to get over it or live like a misery.

It was a funny place to keep a tin bath, anyway, I thought as we went up the stairs. Surely people like these had a wash-house of their own. If the bedroom was upstairs and they kept a bath in it, that did not leave much room for the rest of us. I noted, as she struggled up the stairs in front of us, and you could not see an inch either side, that the old girl was no fairy, and the old boy must take up a foot or two, not to mention Gladys. Perhaps David and I would have to sleep in the tin bath. When we got to the top of the stairs the truth dawned on me. There was a landing full of doors. There was more than one room upstairs. I could not believe it. In our two-roomed tenement everybody lived in one room and slept in the other. You cooked in a little alcove in the corner, ate on the little table pushed against the wall, and sat round the fire on little wooden chairs.

Gladys's mum was talking about whether there was a towel in the bathroom. A special room to put your tin bath in. They must be very well off and posh. It turned out to be a clinic of green and white tiles. The bath itself wasn't tin. It was giant and white and stood on four big iron legs.

"You're old enough to take your own clothes off," said Gladys, but she still did not smile. Her mum stood at the door, and as we took each garment off she picked it up and peered at it through her glasses as if she expected to find something.

Gladys went over and turned on the taps over the bath and water came out. Was she going to stand there and watch? Mum used to watch us in the bath, but I did not know Gladys and I did not fancy her doing it. I looked at David. He looked as lost as I felt. My stomach felt funny. I did not like this place or Gladys and her mum one bit. I felt a bit sick, and I wanted to go home. I wondered how far it was, and whether a boy and his little brother could walk it. I could see Mum cooking the tea on the gas stove in the alcove, smell it, feel the warmth of it. I shivered. Here it was cold, and Gladys and her mum did not look warmer than the house.

We still had our trousers on. The old lady decided she had done enough and turned from the door, booming: "Give them a good scrub, Gladys. You never know where they've been."

I looked down at my thin body. I suppose we were a bit grubby after the train, but I didn't think we were that dirty. Besides, Mum had given us a good going over in the tin bath the night before, just as she did every Friday night.

"Go on then," said Gladys, "get out of your trousers and into the bath."

We both hesitated, then she must have realised why because she went red again, turned off the taps and left the room.

Then I had to laugh, even though I still felt sick. The bath was so tall that David could not get in. I had to push him up by his bum until he got a grip and slithered over the edge and there was a splash. Ten minutes later Gladys came back and turned her head away as we got out. Afterwards we lost ourselves in the stiff newness of the pyjamas Mum had got specially.

The old girl came shunting and grunting up the stairs again. She inspected us. Now we were all fresh and clean she seemed to view us with a bit more pleasure. For a split second she actually smiled, then she just nodded to Gladys.

"You've got the big bedroom," said Gladys, "and the big bed."

She opened one of the doors on the landing and almost pushed us through as though pleased to see the back of us already. It looked as big as some of the fields we had come past on the train, a desert of green lino, and brown and cream paint. There was a mountain of a bed right down the middle, with brass peaks, and a cave of darkness underneath. Just me and David in here? You could have got the whole of the Peabody's flat into it, and perhaps even the wash-house as well.

Gladys had to help us scale up the bed covers. David was first in and she settled him, miles away, it seemed across the brown cover.

When Gladys bunked me up I could see his face over the sheets, and he looked lost and scared.

"I hope you don't sleep with the light on," she almost smiled, looking suddenly pleased at getting us out of the way. "Mother would not like that."

We never had, but then there had always been a thin slit of light under the door into the other room, and you could hear Mum doing things. You knew that any bogy man would have to come through there before he got you. I didn't say anything, because I somehow knew it would not make any difference.

Gladys closed the door, mumbling something about there being a pot under the bed if we needed it. We were prisoners. It was September and it was still light out there through the big windows which overlooked the front gate. I hoped it would stay light for a long time. David had moved in closer.

"Do you like it here?" he said, and I could tell from the way he said it that he was not too keen.

"Not bad." I was trying to be brave like a big brother should.

"Will Mum and Dad be coming down soon?" He tried again.

"Don't know. They said they would when they got a ticket."

Dad was a railway man on the underground, and he was allowed so many free tickets a year. I couldn't help thinking of being home. Mrs Cajegal, the Spanish lady, would more than likely be in our place having a cup of tea. The kids would still be yelling down in the square. The smell would be floating up from Ely's stables right at the back of us, and the horses and the rattling carts would just be coming in for the night.

I tried not to make a noise as the tears started to form in the corners of my eyes. I turned so that my back was towards David.

"I don't suppose we'll have to go to school tomorrow," he said hopefully.

"Be quiet and go to sleep," I said gruffly, not wanting him to realise I was crying.

Chapter II

We did get to sleep eventually, and woke up when the sun started coming through the gap in the curtains.

We lay for a long time just whispering, not knowing whether to get out of bed or not. Eventually Gladys pushed open the door and told us to wash ourselves in the bathroom. Afterwards she came in to see we had done it properly. When she asked if we had brushed our teeth and she found we had no tooth brushes, she ran chattering down the stairs as if this was further evidence of something. David, with his moon face and deep set eyes, looked at me, lost:

"What's she done that for?"

"Don't know . . ."

"How long does a war go on for?"

"Don't know . . . I never remember having one before. I don't expect it's long," I said, trying to sound hopeful.

Just then Gladys started thumping up the stairs again.

"Be quiet," I said, "she's coming back . . ."

Even before she got to the top of the stairs Gladys was boiling out her message:

"Mother says you must have toothbrushes today . . . and a separate flannel and towel for both of you. Come down now for breakfast."

Downstairs the old girl was already in her survey position in the chair, and the man with the one glass in his eye was already hiding behind his newspaper. The table was white with a cloth, broken with embroidered flowers. There was a plate of porridge laid either end, and in the middle were the dishes... milk, sugar, jam, and some orange, stringy stuff. I could not understand it at all. It was a waste. You only dropped things, and somebody would have to wash the cloth, when it was easier to wipe the table. And what were milk bottles and jam jars for anyway if not to hold milk and jam?

We just sat for a while, not knowing where to start, so Gladys reached over and put milk and sugar on to the porridge as if they were gold dust. Both of us were hungry and dug into the thickness of it. It was quite a few seconds before I noticed the look on the old girl's face. Then she tutted.

"You'll have to teach them to eat with their mouths closed," she spat at Gladys. "They've got no manners, no manners at all."

"Well it's not my fault," said Gladys, going red.

"And the noise," said the old lady, "it sounds like a pig sty."

What was a pig sty, I wondered, but by the way she was looking I knew it could not be something good.

They said nothing more until we had cleared our plates and David started licking his spoon. That started the old girl tutting again.

"Come on," said Gladys, pulling David off the chair and towards the back door. She pushed us both through, then stood for a moment with her hands on her hips. I did not like the look on her face.

"You're to play out here. You don't have to go down to the school until the afternoon. Go anywhere you like, but you mustn't go on the lawn, touch the flowers, vegetables or any of the fruit..."

She turned to go through the door and then found something to add:

"And don't make any noise. We don't want the neighbours complaining."

The door exploded behind her. Gladys obviously realised she had got stuck with us, her mother helping only with her mouth. Father would not move out from behind the paper screen.

We looked around the new world. If we were not to go on the grass, flowers, vegetables or the fruit trees, it left us a narrow brown path cutting through the middle of it all. At the top end was a pile of ash where somebody had had a fire. It was not much use right up there, I thought. The place for fires was in big black grates which also cooked the Sunday dinner.

The concrete bit outside the back door was warm with the sun already. The garden was green and smelt like outings to Lambourne End in Essex where we used to go on the Mission bus. But looking around I could not see beyond my fears, and it all looked grey. Besides, it was not as nice as the square at home. On a hot day like this you could sit on the tarred surface, and make patterns in it with your finger tips and dab it all over other kids' noses and faces. The best place in the square was round at the back near Ely's stables and the rubbish stairs. It smelt funny on hot days, but it did not matter. You sat there with your back against the railings round the rubbish stairs and pretended.

The dusty rubbish stairs, with the black door at the bottom, were forbidden to us.

"Don't you ever go down there," Mum said, "you'll catch something."

But eventually the mystery climbed the fear. I remember the first time we went down into the smell we went slowly, afraid that something would jump out on us when we reached the bottom.

The black door was just open, but it was difficult to push it open more. This frightened us a bit, but there were four of us and we kept on pushing. When we got it open wide enough to see in, we found we had been pushing against a pile of rotten scraps, egg shells, fire ash, tins, vegetable peel, and broken china. There were piles of waste everywhere, but they were like little mountains by the two holes in the wall.

So this was where things ended up when you pushed them down the shoot. In Peabody's, each floor had five flats. On each landing there were two lavatories, but you were only allowed to use one even if you were doing it in your trousers; two sinks on the landing where everybody washed and got their water; one big wash-house, which everybody had a right to use one day a week. Under each wash-sink was one iron-flapped covered hole in the floor which everybody called the shoot, and down which everybody pushed their rubbish. It was best when you pushed tins through. They rattled and crashed their way down to the dark room at the foot of the rubbish stairs. Sometimes it was worth taking tins right up to the top floor because the noise was better. Everything not wanted went down the shoot, and the dustman came every so often to clear the mounds down below with shovels.

After the first visit to the shoot room we did not catch anything, so we kept going back, fascinated by the things that ended up there, even digging it over to find better things still.

This posh garden we had been pushed into now did not have any rubbish stairs. David and I wandered up the path, scared to put a toe off it. There was not anything to do. We patrolled the path a few times, not even saying anything for fear of breaking the silence that seemed to typify the whole place. The only diversion were the heads that appeared at one of the house windows from time to time. Sometimes they belonged to Gladys, but more often to her mum.

It was during about the tenth dawdle up the path that David pointed to something under the bushes with the prickly stems. It was not until a thin black thing began to sway behind the main black thing that we realised what it was. A moggy, fat with thick, black hair. Apart from the tail, it seemed to be playing statues. Our first thought was to go and make a fuss of it, and then we saw why the cat was so still. A few feet in front of it, cleaning itself, was a sparrow.

For the first time since we got into the garden, David spoke, but in a whisper:

"Is he going to eat the bird?"

I shook my head. I knew it was wrong for that to happen. In London the birds were our pets. Nobody was allowed a cat or a dog in Peabody's. You could have a bird in a cage and some people did, putting them out on the window ledge on sunny days, flashes of yellow through thin bars.

For most, though, the sparrow and pigeons which ambled and fluttered round the square were all that there was. People even threw out their stale crusts, wetting them first to help the birds. No, the cat must not get the sparrow.

Without thinking, I bent down quickly, picked up a stone from the path and hurled it towards the cat, shouting at the same time. The black bundle jumped and ran, the bird took off. Then there was a shattering sound. We ran to the bit of the path where we could see behind the bushes. There was a funny little house made of glass with plants inside. Right on top there were now two gaps where the stone had brought panes down.

A window opened behind us. In a lighthouse of a movement the old girl took in first the cat now clawing its way up the fence, then the shattered glass.

"What have they done to Pussywillows? Gladys, Gladys . . . those hooligans are out there throwing stones at my cat." Her chins slithered up and down. "You were supposed to be seeing they did no damage."

"Damn your cat, woman, what about my greenhouse?" A second head appeared. It was the first time we had heard the old man say anything.

We gaped at the window, wanting to run, but not knowing where to run to. Then the back door opened, and Gladys came running.

"Come in you two. I'll teach you to get me into trouble." She grabbed each of us by the hair and tugged towards the door. "Upstairs to your room. You needn't think you'll get any lunch either."

"As long as we get some dinner we'll be all right," David whispered to me, not realising that lunch was the same as dinner down here. I had tears in my eyes because I was mad. I knew I had done right. I had saved the bird, hadn't I?

In our room the morning was a long time, but after hours and hours Gladys came and got us. She must have changed her mind, or have been scared of us starving to death or something, because we did get a funny, round shaped egg on a piece of toast. Her mother and father were nowhere to be seen, and had obviously decided they did not want anything more to do with us.

After Gladys had taken us down to the church hall which was supposed to be a school, we realised that she had croaked on us. Mrs Naylor knew all about the Pussywillow and the greenhouse episode, but she gave us both a cuddle:

"You know you mustn't throw stones at cats or greenhouses. You must be careful . . . you've upset your new parents already."

"But miss, we stopped him eating the bird," burst David. "We couldn't go on the garden, we had to throw a stone."

Mrs Naylor just smiled and shook her head. You could tell she was not angry. Lessons were funny. Mainly we just drew and chalked on dark grey pieces of paper. Mrs Naylor said that so far we had no books, but they would arrive soon. Then they kept sodding us about. One afternoon school was in the church hall, another time in the proper school, then next morning it would be out on the downs, wet or dry, because some other classes needed the hall and the school. Mrs Naylor said it was really a lesson, even though we were outside, and that we were studying nature.

One day there was great excitement and everybody was scared when we saw a green snake slithering out of a bank of ivy, but Mrs Naylor said there was nothing to be frightened of because it was the kind that did not hurt anyone. But I noticed she picked up a stick in case it changed its mind. At first it was a change, but then it got boring just tramping over the downs in twos, and we all knew, anyway, that we only had so many nature lessons because there was nowhere else for us to go.

It was during these walks that the bigger boys made up the evacuees national anthem, or said they did anyway. They sang and shouted it everywhere. It made Mrs Naylor laugh at first, but when it seemed to upset the ladies we passed in the street she tried to stop us singing it.

They started by singing the first line quite nicely:

"I know a rotten place, far, far away."

Then they would quickly shove in 'Called Eastbourne', accompanied by a loud boo, before singing again:

"Where we have bread and jam three times a day.

"Egg and bacon never see, never brings us in our tea.

"We are gradually fading away."

David and I tried the song on Gladys once, but she was not very pleased and told us never, never to sing it again. I don't know what she was moaning about. Eastbourne was a rotten place, but then, I suppose, they did not know any better, never having lived in a smashing place like Stepney.

There was an old black tank near the entrance of the park, which Mrs Naylor said was something called a relic of the first war. There had been other wars then. I was quite relieved to hear it. I hadn't remembered a war before, so it meant that they must end sometime. We were allowed to climb over the tank, peer down its gun, and if you were brave enough you could climb down into its smaller black belly. But we did not go inside after the first time: people had been using it as a lav and one whiff was enough.

They were such long days, whatever we did. We had given up crying first thing at night, at least outwardly, but inside there was always this funny pain you knew would not go away until you went home again to Mum and Dad and the square.

Every day I longed for Mrs Naylor to say that the war was finished – at last – and that we would all be going back. It was really only a few days since we'd left London, but to us it seemed like forever.

Things did not improve with Gladys and her mum and dad. Nothing ever seemed to go right. There was the big pole incident. The entrance to the park in front of the downs was just at the end of the road. We were often sent off to play there when Gladys could no longer stop her mother from grumbling about the noise, or our manners, or anything else. Near the entrance to the park were huge, posh houses with white walls and big gardens. We were going past the side entrance of one of these houses one day when we saw a pile of long bamboo rods laid out just inside the open gate.

"Gor, they'd make smashing jumping poles," somebody said. "They're nice and springy."

"They're probably only going to throw them away," somebody else added. "It'd be a shame to waste 'em."

The four of us were quickly through the gate, each pulling a pole upwards. They were about six feet long, but to me the far end of the one I picked up seemed as distant as the moon. I got it upright, but it was so much bigger than I was that it swayed violently and as I tried to walk I kept toppling. The other two boys were bigger but even they were having difficulties. As best we could we staggered the few yards to the entrance. I had not noticed that David was still in there trying to get a pole of his own.

"Quick, quick," said one of the other boys. We all knew, not very deep down, that the poles were not just going to be thrown away, and were scared of somebody coming out of the house.

"Dave . . . come on Dave," I shouted, "leave it, you can have a go of mine."

"No, I want one of me own," he said back. I knew it would take something big to make him give up, and it came at just that moment when a huge old man appeared at the side door of the house, balanced on a pair of walking sticks. The voice was as big as the body:

"Put those back . . . do you hear me. Those belong to my son."

David dropped the pole, and his little white face was soon galloping along beside me, as we all wobbled up the road into the park and behind the bushes at the back of the boys' toilet. We crouched there, giggling and trembling at the same time. The old man was obviously too crippled to have pursued us round the corner, otherwise he would have seen the poles rising high above the bushes, shaking.

After a while we sent David out to see if the old man, or even a policeman, was looking for us.

"I can't see anybody looking," he said doubtfully, still a bit scared by the whole thing.

So we risked it, and went galloping and leaping all over the place, pretending sometimes to be on horses and sometimes, with the aid of the pole, to be champion high jumpers. It was marvellous until we asked somebody the time, and found we should have been back half an hour ago.

"What we going to do with the poles?" said somebody.

"Let's hide 'em in the bushes," I suggested.

"No . . . some rotten sod would pinch 'em. You know what thieves those Eastbourne kids are. We'll have to take them home with us. They're too good to just lose."

After the episode with the stick man I'd have sooner left them, but I did not want to seem different and we all staggered along. I knew we would have trouble when we got back. We were late, and Gladys would be watching for us. We went round the side entrance, and tried to lay the pole alongside the fence where it might not be noticed. When I looked up I realised Gladys had been watching me do it from an upstairs window.

She was down in no time.

"Where did you get that?" The suspicious look she wore most of the time was deeper.

"We found it."

"Yes, we found it," said David. I could see his nose turning up like it always did when he lied. I could always tell, and I was sure Gladys could by this time too.

"Where?"

"Near the park . . . they was just going to throw them away."

She said no more, but turned and called:

"Mum, Dad . . . come here." I knew we were really in trouble. It seemed ages before the other two came out.

"They said they found this bamboo, that somebody was just going to throw them away."

"Nonsense." It was the old man. "Nobody throws away bamboo like that. It costs threepence a foot since war broke out."

"You just took it." Gladys's mum, as usual, thought, and spoke, the worst of us, the quickest.

"It didn't belong to no-one," I said, hoping my nose was not turning up like David's did on such occasions.

Gladys obviously thought the worst too, but, as usual, wanted to avoid trouble.

"I think the best thing is for them to have their tea and then they can take it back to where they found it."

We did not enjoy tea very much, and immediately afterwards Gladys said: "Now you can put that pole back. Off you go."

When we were outside the back door – they never let us use the front – David said:

"What we ganna do?"

At that moment I did not know. We could not go back to the stick man's garden because somebody in the house might see us and, anyway, the two bigger boys would expect us to arrive at the park with our pole again next afternoon. There seemed no solution that would satisfy Gladys and everyone else, but as I struggled to get the pole upright I noticed a drain pipe that ran all the way up the side of the house.

"We'll hide it behind here," I said to David, pushing the pole as close up against the pipe as possible.

"Now quick, outside."

We ran out of the house, and hid round the corner for as long as we thought it would have taken us to get to the park, then went back. When we turned into the side gate, my stomach began to turn over and over. Standing by the drainpipe were the three of them. They looked angry, but half pleased that they had caught us out.

"This time," said Gladys, "I am going to come with you."

So we moved in procession, little David, me, Gladys and the pole. Now there could be no escape. When we showed Gladys the place, she made us stand outside holding the pole whilst she went up to the door.

"Will they fetch a policeman and send us to prison?" said David, obviously sure now that this was going to happen.

"Wait and see." I tried to sound as if I did not care anyway.

At first it was not the stick man who appeared, but a younger one. Gladys was chatting away, nodding towards us, then the young man disappeared for a moment and the stick man came hobbling out.

"Yes, that's two of them," he said. "I saw them this afternoon as they were stealing them."

Stealing them. We had been caught stealing. They came a bit closer and we could hear them discussing.

"Evacuees are they? I suppose you can't expect anything else," said the stick man. "I can't see why they sent this East End lot. It was obvious they would not fit in a place like Eastbourne."

"That's what my mother and father say," Gladys was saying all lady like. "I can only apologise, but we did not choose the children we would get."

The stick man was not satisfied.

"I don't think we ought to let them get away with it. Perhaps we ought to tell the police and teach them a lesson. It might make some of the others watch their step, too."

David had gone white, and even I could almost hear the cell door closing behind me. Bloody Hitler. It was his fault. If he hadn't started the war we would not be in a silly place like Eastbourne and all this would not have happened. Nobody in Stepney would worry about a piece of wood.

It was the young man who saved us:

"Now, now, Dad. I don't think any useful purpose would be served by taking official action. I'm sure this lady will think of some adequate form of punishment."

Even Gladys looked relieved, and she gestured to us:

"Put the pole back and come over here you two."

We did as we were told, but would not go too close. The old man's sticks looked as if they could be painful.

"What do you say to these two gentlemen," said Gladys.

I could not think of anything to say, and there was a long pause. Gladys poked me impatiently on my shoulder:

"Apologise . . . say you're sorry." Then towards the young man, with a thick smile. "They've got no manners at all."

I mumbled something and she ushered us out through the gate, going red. It was worst when we got back.

"They had stolen it," she said to her parents. "They're lucky they're not in the police court and us with them. Then the eldest one wouldn't apologise, and I had to drag it out of him."

"Who did they take it from?" said the old girl.

"Old Mr Evesleigh by the park . . . and him a cripple as well. It was him who wanted to send for the police, but young Mr Evesleigh said it would be better to leave the punishment to us."

The old girl looked at her husband:

"If I were a man I'd give them a good thrashing," she said meaningfully. We looked at the old man, but he did not move.

"Then we'll have to do it some other way. Bryan – you first. Go and stand out in the front garden by the gate. When you get out there say five hundred times – thou shalt not steal. I will be watching and listening from the top window, and I will tell you when to stop."

I went very slowly out to the front gate. It was twilight, but there were still enough passers-by to act as witnesses.

"Thou shalt not steal," I started. It was difficult to say and my six-year-old tongue fell over the words, especially since I was trying to say it quickly to get it over with.

"Say it slowly and loudly. Don't garble it," said the old lady's voice from the window.

As people went by they paused curiously, and some even stopped to stare. I could also hear windows opening, and I shut my eyes so that I would not see the people looking and so that I would keep in the tears of shame and anger that were beginning to form.

"Thou shalt not steal. Thou shalt not steal. Wow shalt not seal. Thou shouldn't swill." Now it was coming out different every time. At last:

"Right you can come in now ... but I think we will give your brother a turn too. There may be hope for him."

David? Out there, with people looking, saying something he would not understand.

I shouted up at the window.

"You old cow you. You dare put my little brother out there and I'll shout and shout until everybody in the street comes out."

To give her a sample, I yelled hard. There was a silence, then she hissed from the window:

"You come in at once."

I did. She did not send David out, and we did not see her again that night. Gladys put us straight to bed.

Afterwards, as we lay there, we could hear raised voices downstairs. Just as I was beginning to fall asleep, David said:

"What's stealing?"

"Just pinching," I said.

Next morning the welfare lady came, the one who had brought us there on the first day. Gladys told us we had been so naughty that they were thinking of sending us somewhere else. I hoped it might be 7A Block, Peabody Buildings, but I knew deep down it would be somewhere here, another prison like this one. If only I knew how to get back I would run away, I thought, and take Dave with me, but I did not even know where to find the green train.

But, anyway, nothing happened. Gladys did not say anything else, and we just stayed on. The old lady said even less to us than before, but one day when she was not looking the old boy slipped each of us a toffee and put his finger across his lips. After that I thought he might understand, just a little. Perhaps he was a prisoner too.

Mrs Naylor must have heard about the pole, but she did not say anything. We were not learning much at school, but one thing was giving us a good laugh. It was now November, and the evacuee school was putting on a play for Christmas about Jesus. There was this doll in a little cot, and some of us were things called virgins, and some angels and some wise men. They made David an angel, and he had to stand behind this doll looking holy with his hands together and a pair of big paper wings stuck on his back. He was quite good at looking holy, and all the teachers said how lovely he looked, but he would not keep still and he kept clouting the Virgin Mary with his wings.

She thought she was very important and did not like David's wings knocking off her veil. One of the boys said it was not really surprising with a face like hers, and that made her cry and hold it all up for ten minutes. The trouble was that the clouting knocked David's wings off and there was another delay while he was made fit to fly again.

I was one of the wise men; unfortunately, the one in the middle. We would just get to the 'orient are' bit when something always went wrong. Either the one behind would step on my cloak, and I would be carrying my frankincense practically naked, or the one in front would stop suddenly and there was a violent collision. Most of the time even the teachers could not keep a straight face, but they tried to look serious and said that we only had a few more weeks before we had to do it all in front of our foster parents. I did not think the old lady or the old man would come, but I knew that Gladys would go back and tell if David did something drastic with his wings on the actual night.

Although it was a giggle doing the play it made us all a bit sad. It reminded us of Christmas. I remembered Christmases at home, and the food and the presents. It made me feel homesick, and I was worried in case Father Christmas did not have our new address. As it got nearer and nearer, I used to slip an extra line into my prayers. And please God let the war end before Christmas so that we can have it at home with Mum and Dad.

God must have been listening, although he did not actually end the war, and he chose a funny way of doing it. I still do not actually know for sure, but I think it came about because, playing out on the downs one day, our control was not good enough.

After a period of being kept in because of the pole, we were let out to play in the time between school and dark. That afternoon we found a hole and decided it must be full of rabbits. There were those little round, black things all over the place that Mrs Naylor called rabbit's droppings when somebody asked her on a nature afternoon, and which somebody translated as just shit.

We got sticks and decided to keep on digging until we captured one. We had got a good way down without actually seeing one of the animals when David started saying he wanted to go to the lavatory.

"Hold it in for a bit longer," I said. "You'd like to catch a rabbit wouldn't you?"

He looked doubtful, but he did not know where the lavatory was, so there was nothing he could do about it. But shortly afterwards I began to feel I wanted to go as well. I still would not give in, and urged David to dig harder. It was only when he began to cry, and there was a strange smell, that I realised we had gone on too long.

"Quick," I said, "let's go to the lavatory in the park."

I grabbed his hand and began to pull him over the grass. We were still only half-way there when it suddenly happened to me as well.

"I wish we had not dug for rabbits," said David.

I cleaned us as best I could, but our trousers and underpants were in a filthy state and the smell was terrible. I thought of Gladys and the old girl, and I wanted to run away, but I knew we would smell wherever we went. Along the road people looked at us strangely as we walked bow-legged towards the house.

The old girl was sitting in her usual chair when we went in. We stood there for a while, but she did not look. Then she began to sniff.

"Gladys, Gladys . . . what is that smell?"

When Gladys appeared she had only to look at us standing heads bowed by the door and the tell-tale brown marks down our legs to know the answer. It was her look of horror that made the old girl look round. She shrieked, and the old boy came in thinking something terrible was happening.

"We was digging for rabbits," I mumbled, "and . . . and . . . we left it too late."

"Oh my God," said the old lady, "I really have had enough of this. They should have taken them last time. Gladys, do something."

Poor Gladys did not know where to begin. Finally she spread sheets of newspaper on the kitchen table, and we had to stand up there in full view whilst we took our soiled things off.

There we remained until the welfare lady arrived to see the proof of our crime.

"You really must stop doing things like this," she mumbled.

"We didn't do it on purpose," I blurted.

"Be quiet," said Gladys.

"Don't you think they had better have a bath?" said the welfare lady turning up her nose.

About an hour after we first arrived home we climbed into the bath. As she gazed at us Gladys looked as if she would never feel clean again.

The next Saturday Mum and Dad came. We did not know they were coming. They just appeared at the back door. Gladys was obviously expecting them: our clothes were in little brown paper parcels.

In ten minutes we were holding our parents' hands as we walked down the street to catch the bus to the station. The thrill of it, the relief of it, to see them again . . and to be going home. I could not say anything. I just kept looking at their faces, not really able to believe that they were there at last.

On the train, I said:

"Is the war over then?"

Mum put her arm around me.

"No, not yet, but they haven't dropped any bombs on London, so we thought you might just as well come home."

That night Mum bathed us in the tin bath in front of the fire in the black stove.

"You never know with these high-class people," she said, "whether they've been looking after them properly."

And I did feel cleaner than I had ever done in Gladys's big white bath in Eastbourne. David even looked cleaner. Good enough to be an angel even without wings. Then I remembered the play, and wondered what they would do without an angel and a wise man, but the Virgin Mary would be pleased at least, I thought, just before I dropped off to sleep against Peabody's beige distemper.

Chapter III

It was lovely being back. It was all over: I would never let them send me and David away again. The square was still there. The pigeons and sparrows still pecked after the soaked bread, though some things were different. At two places in the middle of the square they had put low brown buildings with concrete roofs. Dave and I were both a bit upset about this when we went down to play that first morning: it meant we had to push our tin pedal cars all the way round them instead of cutting straight across. We complained to Mum.

"They're called shelters. You 'ave to use 'em if the siren goes. That means that Hitler's going to bomb us, and we're safer in them places than we are up 'ere. Our shelter's on the ground floor in this block. If you're ever playing in the square when the siren goes you bloody well come straight back to the block."

Hitler would never come. We had been in Eastbourne all that time and he had never come, so he would not bother now. Perhaps he had not meant to cause a war, and was now trying to forget about it.

They had done something in the sky, too. Over the docks it was full of big silver elephants, with flappy ears, attached to the ground by long strings.

"They're barrage balloons," said Mum, "so that, if the German airplanes come they won't be able to get down far enough to do any real damage."

Dinner was sausage and mash and tomatoes, our favourite. Gladys would never give us sausages. Her mother said they were common. It was when we went down again to the square that we first realised. We had been so busy in the morning exploring, making sure that everything was still there, that we had not noticed. There were not any other children about, only big boys or little babies in prams. We were the only ones back. The whole of St Paul's School, apart from me and Dave, was still in Eastbourne. There would not be anybody to play with . . . but what did it matter. We were really here, back in the grey towers of flats, and people who shouted to each other across the street or out of windows and made each other laugh.

They spoke properly, too. Gladys and her mum had told us we did not speak properly and pulled us up whenever we said 'arm for harm or ain't, or almost anything. We kept telling them that everybody spoke like that except the people in Eastbourne, but they still did not like it whenever we opened our mouths.

As we were going to bed that evening, Mum said we must lay-in next morning until she got home. She had started office cleaning at Ibex House in the Minories. She had to get up early, but she would be back by eight to give us our breakfast. Even if we went into the next room we were not to go outside.

"We'll be late for school," I said.

"There ain't no school for you to go to. They're all like St Paul's, closed 'cos the kids are evacuated. Don't know what we're going to do about that."

"Do you have to go to work?" David asked. I think he was still afraid that she would disappear if she left Peabody's and we would have to go back to Eastbourne.

Mum laughed at his serious face.

"I can't let 'em down. We need the money too. Haven't you noticed the things we've managed to get?"

There was a chiming clock on the mantelpiece, and Dad had already put words to it:

"Play up Millwall, can't play football. Oh yes we can, we beat West Ham . . ."

Then the number of dongs was meant to be the number of goals they had won by.

There were also two funny bronze lady statues at each end of the mantelpiece. They were holding flaming sticks above their heads and they were being followed by three dogs apiece. They must be looking for something, I thought.

"And then there's the bed settee," Mum said proudly. "We wouldn't 'ave been able to afford that on just your father's wages."

I had noticed the settee. It meant that now Mum and Dad slept out in the living room instead of us all being together in the bedroom, but that was all right as long as we could see the light under the door.

When we woke next morning they were both gone, but the bed settee was still open. We tried it. We found that the springs made funny noises when you moved about, and that they made even better noises when you stood up and jumped. David was giggling and laughing so much that the tears started to run down his round cheeks. Then it happened. There was a kind of bang and half of him disappeared through the bottom. He still could not stop laughing, even when I had trouble pulling him out.

We were still laughing when Mum's big iron key sounded in the door. I told her what had happened, and at first I thought she was going to be angry, but then she cuddled us both to her and told us not to do it again.

"It's probably only a couple of springs gone anyway," she said, already turning to the gas stove right alongside the bed to start cooking the breakfast. We both knew then that she was pleased we were back and that she had missed us. She was very proud of that settee, too. It looked so brown and shiny when the bed was folded back that it almost looked like a proper one.

It was the next morning before Mum got home that we inv-estigated the chiming clock. We were laying on the bed settee, not daring to jump on it again, when the clock reminded us about itself by bonging. We just wondered how it made the song. Climbing on a chair, I lifted it down. There was a door in the back, and inside that a

row of little hammers. I pulled one back and let it go. It made the
note somewhere between Mill and Wall, and David was so pleased he
laughed.

"Let me do it," he said.

After that we tried to play the whole tune ourselves, pulling back
the hammers as far as they could go. It was lovely, but I thought it
better to get the clock back on the shelf before Mum came in. I had
just managed it when she appeared.

"What 'ave you two been up to this morning?" she said.

"Nothing Mum," said David, his nose turning up again.

We had just finished eating when old play up Millwall started
belting it out again. Only this time something was wrong. It was
distinctly off key and it was missing about one note in three. Mum
looked at us closely, and we were scared to look at her in case we
burst out laughing.

"I'll 'ave to take that bleedin' clock back," she murmured. "It
shouldn't be worn out this quickly."

"I told you not to bend them hammers back to far," I said to
David afterwards as we ran down the stone stairs into the square.

That afternoon Mum took us to the Cable, the cinema in Cable
Street where so much horse hair was coming out of the seats that it
tickled your bum. It turned out to be cowboys and Indians . . . which
was unfortunate for the two ladies and their dogs who were looking
for something on the mantelshelf.

Next morning we tried lassoing them with pieces of curtain wire
laying on our backs on the bed settee. Both fell at almost the same
time, and there must have been a weakness in the making because
both arms holding the flaming sticks broke off at exactly the same
place.

"What we ganna do?" said David, and then suggested we run out
of the buildings so that we would not be there when Mum found out.

I could not think of anything better for some time until I noticed
the box of matches on the gas stove.

"Quick," I said, "you hold the statue while I get two match
sticks."

The first one fell down inside the lady as I tried to get it to stay upright long enough for me to stick her arm and flaming torch on to it. The second one I somehow managed to put in sideways so that enough of it still showed to put the arm on, then slowly, ever so slowly, I climbed the chair and put her back. There was a gap between her arm and her arm hole, and if you touched it the limb wobbled about, but it would have to do. I repeated this with the second lady, and, if anything, her arm was more wobbly than that of the first.

The arms fell off again during the morning when Mum was dusting up there, and David could not stop himself from telling. She was angry with us for the first time since we got back.

"What's the use of me getting up at five o'clock to go cleaning if you break every bleedin' thing we get wiv the money," she said.

I was sorry about it then. I could see she was nearly crying, but she did not make us stand out in the square saying: Thou shalt not lasso statues.

A week later it was Christmas. Granny Breed lived in one of the single rooms on the same landing, but Granny Barclay, Aunt Cissy and Aunt Bindy lived in Wapping and had to come up Nightingale Lane which was really a dirty old valley between dock walls, in which a bird never sang.

When they arrived with their presents they helped us make chains out of different coloured pieces of paper. It was lovely. We had meat for dinner and there was a cake for tea with a little Father Christmas on top. There was only one mishap. Aunt Bindy had a little daughter, much smaller than us, called Joyce, who was always crying about something, and we were always being told not to upset her. This time she was not very happy because she had some skin thing and there were big scabs all over her legs. She and David were arguing about who to sit at one of the little desks Mum and Dad had bought us when it all collapsed and the metal legs took the top off one of the scabs.

Everybody blamed David, and Joyce was dragged out still howling, but Granny Barclay, Aunt Cissy and Uncle Ted stayed to finish the Guinness. Aunt Cissy was a big, jolly woman who worked as a cook, and who had a way with children so that they all quickly loved her, but tonight she was a bit sad.

She had two sons in the navy, and she was obviously wondering what they were doing. Once we had been with her in church before we went away and they had sung a hymn about those in peril on the sea and she started crying and had to go out.

We were getting ready for bed when Mum suddenly asked everybody to be quiet and listen. It was a squeezy old organ, and somebody singing to it.

"Sounds like old Mutton Eye," said Granny Barclay.

"Can't be," said Aunt Cissy. "I heard they'd found him frozen to death on the embankment in front of the Savoy Hotel."

We all went to gape out of Granny Breed's windows which looked out on to John Fisher Street.

"Yes it is," said Mum, "it is old Mutton Eye."

By the entrance to the block a big man sat on the block wall – lucky they had taken away the spikes to make guns, I thought – illuminated by the light from our window and playing on a tiny organ which he worked by pumping at two pedals with his feet. He was shouting 'Silent Night', and it sounded awful.

"Why is he called Mutton Eye?" I said.

"It's because he's only got one and that's crossed," said Aunt Cissy. "He's a sort of tramp, and he gets enough for a night's lodging by singing in the streets."

"God knows how old he is," said Granny Barclay. "He used to come round playing that same organ when I was a girl."

"Poor old sod. I'll get my purse and throw him down a shilling."

As soon as the sound of metal hitting the pavement came, Mutton Eye stopped playing and scrambled about under the gas lamp. Mum's shilling was quickly followed by other coins from other windows, and a few people called out too.

"Happy Christmas, Mutton Eye."

"Piss off to bed. You'll be late for Petticoat Lane in the morning."

"Vot you vant singing hymns like that? Don't you know any decent yiddisher melodies?"

It all ended when an air raid warden came out and shouted: "Put those lights out." And because you could be sent to prison if you didn't, everybody did.

It was only when we were in bed that I thought of all the other kids still in Eastbourne away from their mums and dads, and I suddenly felt sorry for them.

"I wonder what Gladys and her mum are doing now," I said to David.

"I'll tell you a secret," whispered David. "When I wrote my note to Father Christmas I told him not to take anything to them."

"Quite right too," I giggled. I was quite proud of him, and I wished I had thought of that.

We never regretted being back, but there was no school, and, as the winter days passed, the square gradually began to feel big and empty. We were beginning to grow tired of playing bogey men in the shelters, and of shouting 'Nazi' up at Mrs Lear's windows and running away. Mrs Lear was the big German woman with the two fat daughters. It was the biggest one who had the moustache. Everybody started talking about Mrs Lear after it was said she was practising signalling to German planes by leaving her blackout curtains open two inches at night. And somebody else said they had seen the big torch she had ready to lead the dive bombers to the docks when they actually started coming.

"They say she's even got a German uniform hidden away, ready to put on when Hitler's storm troopers come marching down the street," Mum whispered to Dad one day when she thought we were not listening.

Granny Breed said they ought to have taken her away like Jack, the Italian ice-cream man who used to have the barrow under the railway arch.

"They won't intern her because she has been here too long," said Dad. "Jack came only after the last war, but she was here even before that."

After a while, Mrs Lear did not even bother to open her window to see who was shouting Nazi, so we stopped. We even started chasing pigeons, we were getting so bored, until one day something funny happened. We had just been told off for knocking a ball against a block wall, when somebody shouted out:

"Eh, Breedy . . . shit yourself lately?"

When we turned round there was Fatty Farnese and Tiny Turner. They were in another class at St Paul's.

"I thought you were in Eastbourne," I said.

"We was, but our mums said that there wasn't any bombing so we could come back. I 'eard a lot of the other kids will soon be 'ere, too."

"Let's toss-up for sides." There was enough of us for two teams at last. Next day a few more appeared, until a few weeks later the square was a noisy place again, full of shouting and laughing from early in the morning until the caretaker chucked us out at night.

The summer came and, although most of the school was still away, St Paul's started two classes for those who had come home early.

It was good to be back with the smell of the coffee factory and the dusty playground with the ladybirds, but we had only been there a month when the school holidays started, and I was getting a bit worried. I was now seven and I still could not read or write, except for my name in big, spider letters. A lot of the kids who had stayed on at Eastbourne longer could now read the balloons in the comics, and it was getting embarrassing.

Still, you forgot when the sun was hot and Mum took us down to the Tower of London. Its white walls were not much farther than the top of the turning, past the Royal Mint where they made all the money. The Tower had a little beach right down by Tower Bridge, and when the tide was out it became the East End seaside, the mixture of mud and sand covered by buckets and spades and bodies.

"Your grandfather came down from Scotland to build that bridge," said Mum every time we got on the beach, although we had heard it dozens of times before. "That's how he met Granny Barclay."

He and Granny Barclay had parted now. She still lived in Wapping, but he had a dirty old place in the buildings just over the bridge. Sometimes Mum would say we would have to go over the water to see him, and we would all amble over the bridge. Bermondsey was like a foreign country, always referred to as over the water. You did not venture right across Tower Bridge unless you really had to.

The water on the beach was browner than chocolate, but all the kids splashed around in it, and the bigger boys swam out to the barges moored out in the river.

There would always be a bloke with a box strapped round his neck selling water ices. Once or twice when we were sucking away at a Wall's Cube, Mum said:

"You'd never think there was a war on, would you? I don't expect anything will happen now."

It was Dad who kept telling her not to speak too soon, and he was proved right one day in August.

The sirens went while we were playing in the square, and all the kids rushed to their own blocks. Mum was already at the block entrance carrying the gas-masks. It must have been a Saturday because Dad also appeared and started to push us along the passage to one of the doors which had a big 'S' on it. The room was already full, with most of the benches occupied. Everybody was talking at once, and babies were crying. In the end Mum and Dad squashed in and Dave and me sat on the floor.

Mrs Cajegal, the Spanish refugee lady who used to make us carbuncle soup, was next to Mum.

"Kitty, Kitty – he is sending his dive bombers," she said. "It is like Spain."

"Don't worry Mary – we're ready for him. We've had enough bleedin' time to be anyway," said Mum.

"From Spain I learnt something," said Mrs Cajegal. "You must always be ready."

She lifted a big bag from the floor.

"Food. I have had it packed ready. We may be here for days."

"It's probably just a false alarm, or maybe they won't get this far. They said they would sound the sirens when they reached the coast. It could even be a reconnaissance plane making sure we're still here," said Dad.

Now the first shock was over, people began to joke a bit. Somebody noticed the German lady and her two fat daughters, and shouted:

"We'll be all right. The Germans will never drop anything on us with 'er 'ere wiv us. She's bound to have let Adolf know where she would be hiding from the bombs."

Everybody laughed, except Mrs Lear and her daughters, but they were cut short when suddenly the whole place was filled with noise, and the reinforced walls shook. All the windows had been bricked in to keep out the blast and nobody could see what was happening.

Mrs Casey, the Irish woman, was on her feet, walking between the rows with a bottle of water. She took the cork out and started flicking the water over everybody.

"Holy Mary, mother of God, save us from the bombs," you could just hear her shouting above the noise.

"Keep your bloody holy water to yourself," somebody shouted at her, but all the other people, even the Protestants, kept quiet just in case it may have been giving them some protection.

Then one of the men stood up and shouted:

"Now don't worry. Most of the noise is from the ack-ack guns. They're ours, giving them Jerries a pasting. Not much will get past that and the barrage balloons."

Everybody seemed to feel a bit better after that. Some got out the little rubber plugs from their gas-mask holders and shoved them in their ears. Mum shoved ours in – 'to stop your ear drums from being burst' she said – but you could then feel the noise rather than hear it.

The same man who had stood up shouted: "Let's sing."

He started with: "We're going to hang out our washing on the Siegfried Line, have you any dirty washing mother dear."

The only trouble was that those with ear plugs in could not hear properly and they all started singing different songs until there were half a dozen going at once.

It seemed to go on for hours, the singing, the holy water, the guns and Mrs Cajegal jumping up to offer everybody a biscuit. Every so often there would be a deep thud and everything shook and Mum would look at Dad and cuddle us closer to her.

Then the sound of the guns began to die, and it gradually got farther and farther away. Mrs Casey wanted to go out.

"Wait awhile – they may send in a second wave. They'll make sure there's not another lot coming before they sound the all clear.

You'll know soon enough what they've done, and at least we know that this block is still standing."

We sat there, everybody hoping that it was the last of it, quiet to catch the first sound of any new guns or bombs. Then it came: the unbroken wail of the 'all clear'.

Somebody started cheering, and others joined in, pleased to be still alive. They were laughing and joking again.

"They will be coming back again now they have started," said Mrs Cajegal almost to herself as we went out into the passage. "They did in Spain."

Everybody from all the other shelters was out in the street. There was a smell of burning and a lot of smoke, but nothing could be seen in the street for the blocks of flats. Then a procession started back into the block up to the top floor. We pushed into the wash-house.

"Oh my gawd," somebody said, as most just stood silent. "The whole of London docks must be alight. Incendiary bombs – the gits are using fire."

Everywhere there was the sound of fire engines.

"Let's see, Dad," I said, and he stood me on a draining board between two pairs of bloomers hanging from a line.

Even the sky seemed to be alight, and, despite the flames, it seemed to be dark because of the smoke.

"I wonder how many got killed," said Mum, looking at us seriously, and obviously thinking something.

When she put us to bed that night she made us keep our socks and shirts on and put our gas-masks at the bottom of the bed.

"Mum," I called, as she turned down the gas light, "we won't have to go away again will we?"

I could feel her thinking, even in the half light:

"Don't worry . . . there's no need to be worried," she said finally.

But I was, with the thought that if the bombing came again we might be evacuated. I'd sooner be here with the bombs, I thought, than somewhere else safe but away from Peabody's and Mum and Dad. I knew that Mum did not want us to go away, but I was still afraid that the bombs might make her think we would be happier in the country.

Chapter IV

The next morning we found little pieces of jagged metal in John Fisher Street and in the square. We took a few pieces up to Dad, who studied them closely.

"Shrapnel," he finally said. "The papers are full of it this morning. It's little pieces of bomb that fly all over the place when it explodes."

Then, to Mum:

"You see what might happen if you were out in the street when there was a raid on."

Mum did not say anything, but just looked at us in the same way as she had looked in the top wash-house the day before. Dad ruffled our hair and pushed us towards the door.

"See how much more you can find. You can start a collection."

Down in the square the bigger boys were full of it. How it would have been worse but for the Hurricanes and Spitfires which had had dog-fights with the bombers before they reached London. Smelling the smoke still in the air and remembering the fires of the night before, I said that quite a lot must have got through and dropped their bombs. They weren't very happy about this:

"What do you know anyway, Breedy?" One of them said. "My Dad is a fire-watcher and he saw it all. He could see them fighting and firing a long way from London, and he said a lot of the bombers turned back before they got here. He was up on the Co-op roof so he could see for miles."

I still could not help thinking that Hitler must have been quite pleased with all the buildings he had burnt out, but the boy was bigger than I was so I kept quiet. Secretly I wanted him to be right because it might mean that the Germans would not bother again, but I knew my father thought they would keep on coming now they had started.

He was right. That afternoon the siren went again. This time we were indoors so we were quicker down to the shelter and we all got a seat. Mrs Casey had her rosary out this time as well as her holy water. When he got splashed one man told her to keep it to herself:

"We may be in here so long we'll need to drink it," he grinned.

Mrs Casey ignored him apart from hissing something to somebody else about blaspheming.

Mrs Cajegal had brought some carbuncle soup in a jug and some plates and gave us some. When the guns started firing the plates shook so much that the soup splashed the floor, but it was concrete and nobody seemed to mind. This time everybody knew what to expect and there was not the same shock. They just sat with the ear plugs on and started singing automatically.

This time, though, after a while the place started to smell. There were two toilets in little cubicles, but they had no chains, only some white water in their tin bottoms. The day before people had been too scared to use them in case there was a direct hit while they were sitting on them.

"Fancy being found like that when they dug you out," said one old girl.

Today they had got used to it, and everybody was making use of the facilities. The place itself had the stink of cold concrete, and now with the added smell of the filling toilets it really ponged.

At last the all clear went again and immediately people made for the top wash-house again. It looked the same as it did before, but this time there seemed to be more dust mixed with the smoke.

"They're using more explosives with the incendiary bombs," Dad said to another man.

"At this rate," said the man, "in a week there won't be anything left to bomb."

People were beginning to stop Mum in the street. Had she heard about the Morgan family, or the Jacob family, or the McCleod family? All buried alive before they had a chance to get out. The A.R.P. were digging in the rubble to try and find them, but they did not hold out much hope. And at that they would all get out their hankies and have a little cry.

"That's the trouble with living so near the docks," said Granny Breed as she sipped her jug of brown ale fetched every dinner time from the Irish House in Royal Mint Street. "They're bound to go for them, and we're too near for comfort."

I did not mind how near we were, as long as they did not send us away and we could all stay together. The first time it happened at night was a bit scary, though. I thought I was dreaming. I was really asleep but I could hear Dad shouting:

"Wake up, wake up. The bombs are coming in the middle of the night."

I could hear a wailing but could not wake. Then I was picked up and came to in the shelter having my arms and legs pushed into a one-piece thing called a siren suit. Everybody was in their night clothes, and I could see the long underpants of one man sticking down underneath his overcoat.

The Mrs Lear daughter, with the moustache, had her hair in curlers. One of the men whistled at her and she thought he meant it because she went red, then turned away smiling.

"You're all right there," one of the other men said and laughed.

Then the usual bangs and crashes started again. Mrs Casey finished sprinkling her water, assured one or two that it was the only thing that had saved us so far, and then moaned:

" 'Tis a pity we've not got one of them outside shelters like the people in J and H blocks. They have bunks in them and you can get some sort of rest before getting up in the morning."

Everybody laughed at getting any sleep in the noise that was going on, but, as the night raids got more frequent, they had to admit there was something in what she said. The people in the other shelters started going into their bunks at bed-time, and there were just a few who slept through the raid.

"They think they are safe you see, and nobody has to wake 'em up to get them to the shelter," said Mrs Casey when she came to make the point again, as she often did.

I could see Mum and Dad were tired. Sometimes the all clear had hardly gone before it was time for them to go to work. Sometimes David and I wished they did not have to go, but Dad said he had an 'essential' job on the London Transport, so he had to go in no matter what. Mum seemed to hate the thought of Ibex House ever getting a speck of dust on it, even though the office buildings around it had largely disappeared and it itself had hardly any windows left.

I could see, though, that they were getting more and more worried about us. A lot of the other kids had disappeared again.

"What's happened to Fatty Farnese?" you'd ask in the square, after you had not played with a particular boy for a few days.

"He's gone – 'is mother's had him evacuated."

Every time it happened I got so scared I wanted to pee myself. You wondered whose turn it would be next. To make it plain, every time it happened I said to Mum: "Fatty Farnese's gone. You won't have us evacuated will you?"

I think it was only this, her knowing how much we wanted to stay, and her wanting us near her, that outweighed her fears that a bomb might get us.

"Perhaps it is better that we all go together anyway," I heard her say to Dad one day.

"Perhaps we're being selfish," replied Dad.

Two nights later the siren came again.

"It's the full moon," Mrs Levy had said only that morning to Mum, "he would never miss a full moon. It makes it much better for his bombers to see. Better keep your clothes on ready for the shelter."

She said: "Vot did I tell you," the minute we got into the shelter with the sleep still in our eyes and minds.

By this time everybody had their own seats, and we took ours near the door, next to Mrs Casey. The ack-ack guns had only just started when everything went black. Things were falling off the walls and ceiling and people were being thrown about. I finished up under Mrs Casey, and David was on top of her. There were moans and a few screams. It had happened, I thought. We ourselves had been bombed this time. It was difficult to tell what had really taken place until some of the men switched on their big torches and began to shine them round the shelter.

The bricked up fireplace had been blown out into the room, and there were jagged holes where the blocked windows had been. Some people had been hit by the bricks and were bleeding, and the people near the fireplace had suddenly turned negro. The shelter-makers had not cleaned it before they filled it in, and the soot had followed the bricks.

Mrs Casey was already going through her rosary, and I wished she had got off me before she started. Mum dragged us up and wiped some of the dust and soot from our faces to make sure we were not bleeding. You could not hear the noise of the bombing for the babies' crying and the people screaming. A man in a tin helmet appeared at the door.

"K block's had a direct hit," he shouted. "We need some help." K block was the throw of a tennis ball away. No wonder the bricks had blown in.

The men rushed out.

"Dave, be careful Dave," Mum called at Dad as he went.

Mum and some of the other women brought bowls of water from the outside sink and began washing faces and finding the cuts. There were some nasty ones, Mum said, but nobody had to go to hospital. The first aid kit in the shelter coped. Then everybody sat and waited to hear what had happened to the people in K block. Everybody knew somebody who lived in it, and most of them would be in the shelter under it like we were.

"Gawd help them" said Mum, and Mrs Casey said a Hail Mary. It seemed hours before the men came back. They were filthy and their hands were bleeding from pulling at rubble. They were too shocked to speak at first, and Dad could not look at us. He had been sick and there was some still down the front of his dungarees.

"Sliced in two...the whole block just sliced in two," Mr Levy said.

"One of them new aerial torpedoes," said somebody else. "They did not stand a chance."

"Mother of God . . . how many got out?" said Mrs Casey.

Mr Levy shook his head, and that started the women crying and the men turning away. Most of them were still snivelling when the all clear went an hour later. When we were in bed I could hear Dad talking. It was finding an arm with no body attached to it that had made him sick. They had found lots of bodies, babies and women among them.

"It was a direct hit," I heard him say. "It will take days to find the rest of them."

Next morning the square was blocked off. Only one side of K block still stood. Half floors hung down and the window spaces were empty like blind eyes. The rest of the block was a mountain of bricks, being climbed and picked at by the rescue squad. Every so often they would cover something with a blanket and carry it to one of the waiting ambulances.

"Come in," said Mum, "you'll only be in the way." We both knew she really did not want us to see.

Days later there was one big funeral, and the vicar from St Paul's and the priest of All Martyrs R.C. Church said prayers over the empty space that used to be K block. I found out later that they never did find everybody. They had had to give up and just fill in the hole. A hundred and five had gone in one way or another.

The night of the funeral Dad said:

"It's no good. For their own sakes they will have to go again. Look at the children that went with K block."

"But I'd sooner have 'em with me," said Mum, her eyes filling with tears.

"Please, Dad," said David, "let us stay. We don't like being away. We don't mind the bombs. They're funny."

He was too young to realise.

"If they evacuate us again, I'll run away," I said. "They're all like Gladys and her mum, I know they are."

"All right, all right," said Dad, "we'll talk about this later."

Next morning it had all been decided. We would go to Uncle Bob, Mum's brother, and Aunt Maud who lived at Park Royal.

"It's still London," said Dad, "but it is away from the docks."

I still did not like leaving Peabody Buildings, but we would all be together at least. The house in Park Royal was considered a bit posh, even by Mum. Uncle Bob worked for Guinness's brewery and the house went with the job. It had only three bedrooms and since he had three daughters named Maud, Jean and Sally, it was all a bit of a squash.

He was a nice man who was a family hero because he had been in the First World War and there were coloured photographs of him in uniform and Royal Artillery badges in the front room. It was Aunt Maud who could be a bit prickly, especially when she thought Uncle Bob had taken a drop more than he should.

The first few nights when the siren went we all tried to get into the Anderson shelter that had been dug in the garden. Since it had only been made to take two or three at the most, it was impossible. Nobody slept, and everybody was grumpy.

There was a big electricity pylon at the back of the little garden, and Mum kept asking what would happen if it got hit and fell on the Anderson, which did not help.

David and me were not helping at all, as usual. Aunt Maud insisted on keeping an emergency supply of food and drink in the Anderson shelter, and one nibble led to another. A week after we arrived it was suggested we took a bundle of blankets and spend our nights in the shelter of the Brylcreem factory, half a mile away along the North Circular Road. It was made of solid concrete and was so tall that they could put three bunks on top of each other. David and me would share the top one, which was great because you could pretend to be asleep and watch everything that was going on. It was difficult to sleep anyway. One man had a piano accordion which he played most of the time and kept on at everybody to sing.

There was no school we could go to. Mum wanted us out of the house as much as possible to keep Aunt Maud from getting upset, and most of the time we roamed the streets shrapnel-picking. There seemed as much around Park Royal as there was around Stepney, but I did not tell Mum that in case she decided it was just as dangerous.

One of our biggest problems was Sally. She was eleven and had been told by Aunt Maud to watch us, and she did a thorough job. She was near enough to our age to argue with, and everything we did got back to her mother. We had a fight most days, and it ended up with Jean or Maud having to separate us.

The biggest fights were about the canal. We had been told that we should not go near it, but when we could shake off Sally we invariably did. It was the only decent thing around. Tin cans became battleships, and we tried to sink them from the towpath with stones. We went there once too often. We thought we had lost Sally, but when we got back Aunt Maud and Mum knew that we had been to the forbidden place. She had obviously followed us, and then gone back to tell.

"What have I told you about going to the canal," shouted Aunt Maud. "You'll finish up getting drowned . . ."

Half-way through, Mum started siding with us, and it turned into a row. I finished up by calling Aunt Maud 'All mouth and trousers' and being sent to the Anderson. I immediately ate the emergency supplies out of spite.

Next day we took the blankets back after spending the night at Brylcreems, and then walked to the bus stop with our suitcases. We were going back to Peabody Buildings. I think even Mum was pleased, but she told us off for upsetting Aunt Maud just the same.

Chapter V

They had put concrete down and tarred over where K block used to be. Nobody would ever have known that it had been there except for a little altar which had been made out of orange boxes. There was a cloth on it, a statue of the Virgin Mary and a bunch of flowers.

"I don't think that's right," said Mum. "They wasn't all Catholics."

"The bomb didn't make any distinctions," said Dad.

Mum seemed worried about K block. She would go into Granny Breed's room, where you could see it better, and just stare down at the empty space.

The next afternoon and the next night there were raids again. They had patched-up the shelter, but plaster and dust kept coming down every time there was an explosion. One of them seemed almost as near as the K block one, but the window bricks stayed in this time. Next morning we found out it was a whole block of Katharine Buildings, just across the railway arch from Peabodys.

"Another eighty gone," said Mum.

It was the same morning that she asked Granny Breed to keep an eye on us and disappeared towards Cable Street.

She did not say where she had been when she returned, but she was very quiet. She left it to Dad to tell us while she had a cry in the bedroom. Even he could not look at us.

"You can see what is happening," he said. "The raids are still going on. It is too dangerous for you to stay in London. For your own good you must go to the country. We would never forgive ourselves if something happened to you when you could have been somewhere safe.

"Mum went and saw the evacuation organisers at the school in the Highway this morning." So that was where she had gone. "There is a special train tomorrow."

We had a bath in front of the fire, and Mum did not stop snivelling. Afterwards she put two of everything into a little suitcase. She made us sandwiches, even though she knew they would give us some before we left the Highway.

"Do we really have to go?" I asked as she tucked us into bed. She just nodded and turned away. Her eyes were swollen and red.

I awoke next morning before it was light. Dad was in his working clothes bending over the sleeping David and giving him a kiss. I quickly closed my eyes. I did not want to cry. I felt him bend down and his lips on my forehead.

"God bless," I heard him whisper.

Back in the living room he said:

"Don't go crying in front of them. It will only make it worse."

When Mum came in to wake us she could see I had been crying but did not say anything. She cooked a good breakfast, but I could not eat much.

"You must eat something. It may be hours before you get your next meal," she said, despite the two big packs of sandwiches which stood on the table. David ate his breakfast, but even he ate more slowly than usual.

"Where will we be going, Mum?" asked David.

"They could not say for certain, but it will be somewhere nice, I'm sure, with fields and cows and things," she replied, not looking at him.

"Who cares about cows," he grumbled.

Mum did not say anything at all as she bustled about. I knew she was trying hard to make it all seem normal. She helped us on with our macs, and checked that the gas-masks were in their cases before putting them over our shoulders. Granny Breed came down to the block door to see us off and pushed a penny into our hands.

"It won't be for long, you'll see," she said.

"How the bloody hell do you know?" I thought.

Mum came with us to the school in the Highway which was the evacuation point. There were lots of other kids now waiting to be sent away, but it did not help that funny pain inside, something I had not felt since we were in Eastbourne. Mum booked us in with a man sitting at a table all on its own in the middle of a classroom, then she drew us to one side.

"I'm going now. You be good . . ." She could not finish and hurried away out of the school entrance.

David called her, and wanted to run after her, but I gripped his hand.

"You can't," I said. "We have to stay here and wait. It's for our own good, you heard Dad say so."

"It ain't no good at all, and I don't wanna go," he said as he started crying.

I gave him one of the sweets Mum had pushed into my mac pocket. He sucked at it, but he was still crying.

This time they took us to Liverpool Street Station in buses with brown paper all over the windows to keep the glass in if there was a bomb. We did not know anybody. None of the kids were from Peabody Buildings, and the grown-ups were strangers.

We went straight on to the train, and ten of us were counted into a compartment. The others were arguing about who would sit by the window, but I did not care. David had stopped crying, and I kept him amused by showing him the pictures of places which were above the seats. Unfortunately, there was one of Southend where we sometimes went for days out and holidays, and he remembered and started snivelling again. I opened up the pack and gave him a sandwich, and he stopped.

When the train started, the kids began to talk:

"Anybody know where we're going?" said a bigger boy who had

gained one of the window seats, and when everybody shook their heads, he added wisely:

"The usual cock-up. You just goes and you don't know where you are until you get there. It's bleedin' amazing to me they don't lose more of us. They'd never know, you know."

It turned out everybody had been evacuated at least once before, and that made me feel better, even if I did still have that pain inside.

"They ain't gonna boss me around, whoever they give me to," said the boy by the window who looked as if he had not washed that day, had a tear in his shirt and whose name turned out to be Sullivan. "They tried it at the last place they sent me. This farmer tried to make me get up in the morning and help with feedin' the cows. Do ya know wot I did? I soon put a stop to that. I found some distemper and painted the bleedin' cows green. They had to send me 'ome after that."

"Yeh, I know," said a girl, "they only wants ya for the money they get for looking after ya, and they're always sending ya on errands and wantin' ya to do things for 'em."

Nobody seemed to have been happy.

"The second time they evacuated me," said Sullivan, "they put me with a bleedin' vicar. I was supposed to go to church twice on Sunday, and he read the Bible to me every day, and tried to make me stop swearing."

He grinned. "Well, he could bleedin' try, couldn't he? Even he had to let me go in the end. I found out where he kept the communion wine, didn't I? There was never none left for Sundays, and the villagers complained, so back I come again to the smoke. This is my third time. Well, they can try, can't they?"

The journey was much longer than the Eastbourne one, and I had to take Dave along the corridor to the toilet three times. Out of the windows there was nothing but fields, and Sullivan got so bored that he put his hand up a girl's skirt and had a fight with her brother. A bloke heard the noise and came along the corridor to stop it. He obviously knew Sullivan, and pulled him out of the compartment by the strap of his gas-mask case.

"I might have known it was you," he said. None of us ever saw

Sullivan again, and later I often wondered whether they had done away with him.

Then we scoffed our sandwiches, throwing the crusts at each other. It was not long after that the train stopped at a country station and we all rushed out into the corridor to see some of the kids get out. Everybody cheered and then made rude noises, and the ticket collector and the station porter looked as if they were going to throw a fit.

"Will we be next?" asked Dave when the train wheezed off again.

"Don't ask me," I said. "I don't know everything, ya know."

Every time the train stopped we got up, half hoping, half dreading it was our turn. It was the fifth time the train stopped that a lady came and said that we might as well get rid of this little lot.

Nine of us got out on to the platform, and were immediately pushed towards another of those tall ladies in the green uniform. As she was looking us over doubtfully, the train started up again, and somebody on it shouted:

"Don't bleedin' smile you might split yer face."

She obviously heard because she gave the train a terrible look as it went by. Then she came round taking our names. She did not seem to notice when one boy said his name was Roy Rogers. As we were waiting outside the station, somebody asked her where we were.

"This is Attleborough, but only some of you will stay here. Most of you will be living in villages a little way from here." She talked in a funny way, like a posh country yokel.

"Where's Attleborough, then, and how far is it from the smoke?"

"It's in Norfolk, and it's a hundred miles from London, so you don't have to worry . . . you'll be perfectly safe here. We haven't had a bomb yet."

It was not the bombs that worried us, I thought. It was the hundred miles. And where the hell was Norfolk? I had never heard of it before. It sounded so far away, I wished we had all lived in K block and it had ended then.

But then came a distraction which made us forget for a moment. A car drew up, and David and me and two others were pushed into it. We had never been in a car before. We had seen a few in London, of course, but we had never ever had a ride in one.

"You're all going to Rockland," said the green lady through the window as we started off.

Attleborough did not look too bad – for one thing, it had a cinema which looked a bit like the Cable – but there was not a lot of it. We were soon out in the country again going along a narrow road. The driver did not say anything.

"How far is this Rockfield place?" I asked.

"It'll be a bit more than five mile," he said without taking his eyes from the road.

"Do ya know who we'll be living wiv?"

"You must na ask me things like that," he said. "I'm just the taxi driver, and I've got to take you to the Wesleyan Chapel hall. After that it ain't nought to do with me."

"Wot are the people like?"

"They're all right once you gets to know 'em . . . but it takes time," he laughed. "Aye, it takes time – and I don't reckon you'll be around long enough."

Despite what he said, the three people waiting outside the place that was a church, but did not look like one, seemed all right. They smiled and put their arms round our shoulders.

"So you're our new little guests. You'll do fine. I expect you'll be missing your mothers and fathers, but we'll try and make up for that."

It was the first time I had heard anybody acknowledge that evacuees might not want to be away from home.

I later found that she was Mrs Allen who, with her husband and an assistant, ran the ironmongers shop out on the Attleborough Road. She turned to the short, stout woman.

"I think it would be best if you had the two brothers. Since you've room for two they can stay together. This is Mrs Webster. They've got three children of their own so you won't be short of company."

Mrs Webster had a lot to say, and in the quarter mile we walked through the village she practically told us her life story. Her husband had worked for Mrs Allen as their shop assistant. He was not away in the army because he was a Methodist and something called a conscientious objector. They had let him stay as long as he became an auxiliary fireman. He did not mind saving life, but he would not take it, she said. He did his duty in Attleborough but he was home some part of most days. The Websters' house was a country cottage on the main village street, right alongside the village's six council houses. There was a big garden, and opposite there were just fields.

"This is our home," said Mrs Webster. "Tea will be waiting for us."

And it was: a great table spread with cakes and pies and a loaf of bread and pots of home-made jam of different flavours. A kettle was boiling on an open fire. Standing round the table were the Webster children: Jennie, who was 15, Brenda, 12, and Brian, who was 8, a year older than me. They seemed more shy of us than we of them, but they did not seem to mind us being there.

"You'll need to wash your hands, and then you can sit down to your tea," said Mrs Webster. "Come into the kitchen."

It was a great barn of a room with a red stone floor, and big coppers for doing the washing in. The sink was under the window.

"I'd better help you out this first time," said Mrs Webster. "I expect you're used to taps at home. We have to pump our own water here."

Instead of a tap there was a thick pipe coming up out of the ground with a spout one side and a handle the other. Mrs Webster picked up a bowl, held it under the spout and jerked the handle up and down. There was a creaking and groaning and then water was coming out of the spout.

"Can I do it next time?" said Dave, carried away by it all.

"You won't find purer water than that," said Mrs Webster smiling at our reaction. "It comes from a well right under the house."

When we went back into the room the Webster children were already sitting down, and their mother sat us among them. We goggled at the food. We were being rationed in London, but they did not seem to be going short here. Mrs Webster seemed to know what we were thinking:

"We make most things ourselves. We have fruit trees for the jam, and I make enough to last the year, and the garden provides all our vegetables. Right, now we can start . . ."

Both Dave and me shot out a hand for a slice of bread, and it was back on our plates before we noticed that nobody else had moved. For the first time there was a sharpness in Mrs Webster's voice:

"We always thank the Lord for the food first. Jennie, you'll do it today."

They all bowed their heads and Jennie said:

"For what we are about to receive may the Lord make us truly thankful."

"Now you can start," said Mrs Webster. "I expect you'll soon get used to our ways."

It was alright after that, except that both Dave and me licked the jam knives before putting them back into the pot and I noticed Mrs Webster frowning and the children looking at us then at each other.

Our attic room was up two narrow flights of stairs. It was small but cosy.

"Do you say your prayers?" asked Mrs Webster when she had helped us into our pyjamas and into the bed. Mum sometimes used to sing something, but I did not know if it was a prayer.

Jesus bids us shine (it went), with a cool, clear light, like a little candle burning in the night. In the world is darkness, so we must shine, you in your small corner and I in mine.

I did not like to say it in case it wasn't a prayer so I shook my head.

"Well, I'll say one for you," smiled Mrs Webster, "until you've learnt a few. Tomorrow you had better write a note to your mother to let her know you've arrived safely and where you are."

Then she kissed us both and turned down the oil lamp.

She was certainly an improvement on Eastbourne Gladys and her mum, but I still ached inside, and there was only one place I wanted to be, even if it did mean sitting in shelters most nights and some of the days. I always had this terrible thought that usually came at bed-time: what if Mum and Dad died, and we never saw them again, and we had to stay here for the rest of our lives?

"I think I like this better than Eastbourne," said David, before his eyes closed, "but I wish Mum could be here with us."

Next morning we saw Mr Webster in his fireman's uniform. He was a tall man, and he wanted to know if we were church or chapel. I did not really know, and could only say that we had sometimes gone from our school to St Paul's in Dock Street.

"That sounds like church," he said.

I did not see what difference it made, but later on, when he took us to the Wesleyan Sunday School, I discovered how important it was to him. He ran the Band of Hope, and preached too.

After that, Mrs Webster gave us two pieces of paper and a pencil each.

"You sit in the front room and let your mother know you're all right," she said.

When she came back half an hour later I had drawn a picture of a house with flowers all round it and written my name underneath. David had drawn a cow that looked like a dog with horns. Mrs Webster laughed.

"But you haven't written anything," she said.

It was only when we kept looking down at the table that she realised.

"I don't expect there's been too much time for school with all them bombs," she said. "I'll send these pictures and a note to your mother from myself."

Brian and Brenda Webster had to go to school, but we did not go with them. Mrs Webster took us round the garden.

"You'll have to learn how things grow now you're in the country," she said, but the best thing she showed us was the goat. It was white with a beard and was kept on a chain down at the end of the garden. It did not mind being stroked at all.

"That milk you had in your tea this morning came from Mildred," she said, pointing to the bag under the animal.

They looked like tits to me, not Mildred's, whatever that was, but I did not say anything.

It was a nice house. Even Dave said so. The only funny thing was the lavatory. There was a high box with a hole cut in the middle, but there was no water and no chain. It was so high that every time Dave wanted to go I had to lift him up. When you did it everything went into a big bucket underneath.

When the two youngest Websters came home from school Brian

was told to play with us. He showed us how he milked the goat, and David went 'ugh' and said he wasn't ever going to drink milk if that was where it came from. The trouble came afterwards when Brian started to sound like his father.

"Do you go to church?" he asked, his thin face very serious.

"Sometimes," I replied for both of us.

"You'll have to go to chapel now you're here. I heard Dad say so."

"I'm not worried," I said, truthfully.

"Are you going to smoke or drink when you grow up?" he went on.

"I might."

"Then you won't go to heaven," he said spitefully.

"How do you know?"

"My Dad said so, and he preaches in the chapel so he ought to know." And he poked his tongue out.

I was about to punch him in the eye when Mrs Webster called us for tea.

The next morning Mrs Webster took us to a little hall with a corrugated iron roof. She explained that the hall belonged to Rockland All Saints. There were really two villages, though you could not see the difference. One was called Rockland All Saints, the other Rockland St Peters, because they had churches called that. There was only one vicar who kept both places going by holding a morning service at All Saints and then jumping on his bicycle and puffing two miles, mainly uphill, to do the same thing at St Peter's.

"Neither parish, you see," said Mrs Webster, "will give up its church. But we're chapel so it don't make no difference to us."

It was only when we went inside the hall that I realised that there were more evacuees in the village. At least twenty of them, of all ages, were sitting round the hall as if they were waiting for something to happen.

"Teacher not come yet then?" said Mrs Webster to the two bigger girls nearer the door. "Well, I must be off, so I'll leave my two with you. This is David and Bryan. Just tell him, when he arrives, that they're with me, Mrs Webster, but I expect he already knows."

We turned out to be the youngest there and the girls made a right fuss of us.

"Where'd you come from then?" they said. When we told them, we were in.

"You're one of us then, ain't ya? Most of us is from the Mile End Road and Stepney Green, wiv just a few from Bethnal Green and Bow."

They explained that we had to come here instead of to the proper village school because it was already crowded and they said that evacuees mostly needed special attention anyway.

"They make it sound as if we need our 'eads examined," said Rosie Marsden, one of the girls Mrs Webster had first spoken to.

Just then a short, fuzzy haired man with glasses came in.

" 'Ere sir," said Rosie, "we've got two new ones."

The teacher just smiled. "They look a bit better than you lot, but I expect they're just monsters underneath like the rest of you," he said, but he sounded as if he did not really mean it, and everybody laughed.

He put our names on the register, and while he was doing it explained that his name was Jones and that he was not one of the locals but had been sent up specially from London to teach the evacuees.

"We're happy as can be here, so you've nothing to be afraid of. If you've got any problems about anything, just let me know, won't you?"

The first thing he did was to make everybody push the tables back, and then to jump up and down flinging their arms about.

"Repeat after me," he kept shouting as he himself bounced, "healthy bodies mean healthy minds."

It did not take long after we had all finished panting for him to find out what he had taken on when he put us on the register.

"First, we had better try and discover how much you know," he said. "Sit over there with this piece of paper and write down all you can about dogs."

Dave immediately started to draw but he was mixed up because he put horns on it again. Being bigger, I thought I ought to try and write something. I just put down all the words I had picked up by accident, some of them from walls, hoping that some might be connected with dogs.

"Dags is booms . . . miss naylor . . . bomb . . . German . . . blitz
. . . mum . . . dad . . . granni . . . david . . . bryan . . . breed . . .
evaacuee . . . fotbill . . . shit . . . lurrie . . . schol . . . hetler . . . cri . . .
teef . . . balls . . ."

I felt quite pleased with myself. I was not aware I could write so
many words. When Mr Jones looked, he just shook his head, and as
he turned away, I thought I heard him say 'Poor little sods', but I
knew teachers did not swear so he could not have done.

I could add up 2 and 2 and afterwards Mr Jones said we had not
done too badly at all, but he would have to help us a bit more with
our reading and writing. And so it started.

D . . . o . . . g spells dog. P . . . e . . . n spells pen. C . . . a . . . t
spells cat.

"The cat sat on the mat," Mum used to say, "and blew a hole
right through it."

I told Mr Jones and he laughed, and said they must have big cats
round our way.

When we got home from school on the Wednesday Mrs Webster
said that we were in for a treat. "It's magic lantern night at the Band
of Hope."

Mr Webster went early to get ready because he was showing the
slides, and he saved us six seats in the balcony of the chapel, although
I noticed the place was hardly overcrowded. There was a white sheet
pinned up at the front. Mr Webster stood in front of it while he told
us to open our hymn books and sing number 288. I shared a book
with Jennie, and I liked being close to her. She worked in the village
general store and had a fresh smell of carbolic soap mixed with bacon
and butter and paraffin. Then, while we were singing, Mr Webster
ran round turning down the lamps, until the only light left was the
little flame in the lantern.

"This is the story of a man who let drink get a hold on him," he
said as he pushed in the first slide. On the white sheet a man had
appeared. He had a big, red nose and he was sitting holding a mug
which had the letters 'beer' written on it. Then Mr Webster kept
pulling the slide in and out, and it made the man's arm jerk the mug
to his mouth again and again. It looked funny, and I giggled, but

Jennie poked me to tell me to stop. Mr Webster also pulled the next slide in and out so the man looked as if he kept falling down and picking himself up.

It was a very sad story. Because of the man's drinking, Mr Webster said, he could not pay the rent and his wife and six children were thrown out into the snow. The last slide showed the man behind bars looking very sorry for himself. When Mr Webster had run around turning up the oil lamps again, he asked people to come forward and sign the pledge. Two girls got up and wrote their names in a book that was open on the table at the front, and Jennie whispered to me that they were promising never to let drink touch their lips. I wondered why Granny Breed's daily jug of brown ale from the Irish House had not got her thrown out into the street.

"Did you enjoy that?" asked Mrs Webster as we walked home in the dark. I just said yes, but I was really thinking that it was not as good as the Cable.

Every night when he was in bed, David asked when he would be going home again, and sometimes I would hear him snivelling, after I had said I did not know. I knew how he was feeling. The pain inside was less, and Mrs Webster was alright, but I knew that Rockland would never be as good as Peabody Buildings, nor Mrs Webster as good as Mum.

David cheered up a bit when the first letter came from home, and there were lots of kisses along the bottom and a two bob wrapped up in paper for us to spend. Dad had written it – Mum wasn't very good at writing – and Mrs Webster read it. He said he hoped we were behaving ourselves. He was sure Mrs Webster was very nice, and he hoped that we were helping to milk the cows. He had obviously not heard about the goat.

He said Granny Breed was all right and hoped the war would end soon so that we could come back and get her jug filled at the Irish House. Mrs Webster frowned at that, but did not say anything. She said she would keep the two bob and give us a penny a day to spend at the village shop.

At school, Mr Jones made us work at our reading and writing and that distracted us from thinking about home for a while. He gave us books with pictures in and words underneath, and when he was teaching somebody else he made the bigger girls go through them with us. He even let us take the books home, and we showed off by reading the words to Mrs Webster. Only Brian Webster did not seem impressed:

"I did them books when I was five," he said.

Mrs Webster told him to mind his manners and to be quiet. She was very fair, and treated us the same as her own children, most of the time. The only thing I did not think she was fair about was bath night. They had a tin bath like we had at home, but bigger. When me and Dave undressed and got into it, everybody stayed in the room, even Brenda and Jennie. We were allowed to stay in while Brian Webster had his scrub, but we were sent out when it came to Brenda and Jennie's turn. I was a bit embarrassed about them seeing my thing, but I would not have minded so much if I had been allowed a sample of them in return. In fact, I thought I would quite like to see what Jennie was like. I liked her, and I loved her when she made a fuss of us, pulling us to her already ample bosom.

"I don't think your Mum's being fair," I said to her one day. "She lets you look at us when we're in the bath, but she won't let us see you."

She said: "Why you rude thing you. Fancy you wanting to look."

But I think she was pleased really, because I could see she was smiling as she turned away. I knew she would not tell her mother.

Having a separate school kept us apart from the village children, and at first there were a lot of fights. The Rockland kids used to chant after us:

"Evacuees . . . evacuees . . . bound to have fleas."

They usually did it when there were two or three of us, but when we told the others they waited on them from school. It got so bad at one stage that Mr Jones had a visit from the vicar and his bicycle. Afterwards, Mr Jones told us that if he caught anybody fighting there would be trouble, and it quietened down a bit after that.

The belief that evacuees might be breeding their own personal livestock was not always confined to the children. I realised this the day Mrs Webster gave us threepence to get our first haircut in the village. The man who did it worked on the land, but on Saturday he put a kitchen chair in his stable and became the village barber. When it came to our turn, there were two other men waiting. As he was pushing the clippers through David's hair, these two kept leaning right over.

"I saw three of them run out then. You wait and see – there'll be more. It's just like harvesting . . . as he gets to the middle they'll all be escaping . . ."

And the others burst out laughing. When I got in the chair they kept stamping their feet on the ground as if they were killing things.

Perhaps that was why we paired up with the Council house kids. They, too, were rumoured to do their own breeding. They talked funny, but they were all right. The first day we played with them I asked one of them what he was going to have for dinner. He said 'soap'. I was going to bash him because I thought he was taking the mickey, but he kept on saying it until I realised he meant soup.

At school, Mr Jones was giving us books with fewer pictures and more words, and he said we would soon be up to standard. One of his treats was to read us bits from a book called *King Solomon's Mines*, always on a Friday afternoon. It was exciting and it was the only time everybody was quiet . . . but he never finished it. One Monday morning we arrived at the tin hut and Mr Jones did not come. We were there for hours before the vicar came pedalling up the road and told us that Mr Jones had been called back to London unexpectedly. We would have to go down to the village school.

"The village school? That's a bit of a come down," said Milligan.

We made the fifteen-minute walk down to the school last for nearly an hour.

"I knew the police would catch up with old Jonesey in the end," said one of the boys.

"He's all right. Some of us would have been in a bit of a mess without him," said somebody else. Remembering our first day, I said proudly:

"He taught me and my brother to read and write."

We were all a bit scared of the village school, though nobody would say so. I was particularly worried. I knew Mr Jones had been pleased with my reading, but, remembering Brian Webster, I did not know if we were on the same books. I did not like the thought of being laughed at. But after the first day I knew there was nothing to worry about: Mr Jones had done us proud. Both David and me were up to standard, as he said, and could read almost as well as any of the village kids in the class. In fact, I was really quite pleased to be in the school. The Council house kids were present, and there were more kids of my age—especially girls. There had been a shortage of them in the evacuee school.

Sitting two desks away was a thin girl, with long legs, long fair hair, and blue eyes. Everything about her seemed longer, even her eyelashes. I only had to look at her for a few seconds to make myself fall in love for the first time. I was eight, and it seemed to be time I did. Her name was Betty.

I kept looking at her, but she just blushed and looked away, and I did not really know how to proceed from there. She spoke nicely, and said please and thank you when the teacher spoke to her. Perhaps she would not want to be the girl friend of an evacuee. On the second day she let her eyes meet mine for a few more moments before looking away, and I began to feel there might be some hope for me.

She lived in a house just across the road from the school. I knew, because I watched her walk sedately across to it looking like the picture of Alice in Wonderland in the last book that Mr Jones had given me.

It was on the third morning that my chance came. We had organised games in the playground, and Mrs Banks, the teacher, decided we would play the farmer wants a wife. It was a new game for the evacuees, but I soon saw it had possibilities.

A boy was chosen to be in the middle as the farmer, and the others held hands and circled round singing:

"The farmer wants a wife, farmer wants a wife.
Hey, aye adeyo, farmer wants a wife."

Then the boy picked a wife, and then the farmer just had to have a child, dog and so on. The third time round Mrs Banks decided I was good farming material. As they went round I looked at Betty, but she just gazed at her feet as they went round. I realised she knew what was going to happen. When they stopped, I went over and took her hand and led her to the centre. One of the other girls said:

"We know you now, Betty . . ."

They all laughed, and Mrs Banks told them not to be so silly. We had to put our hands together and whisper to decide who we wanted as our child, and she smelt clean and nice. We chose Dave, and he did not like it because I think he fancied himself as a full-grown farmer. As we were choosing our dog, I whispered whether I could talk to her at playtime, and she smiled shyly and nodded her head. David said: "Ugh!"

She was waiting in the corner by the toilets, and I did not know what to say to her. "I'm an evacuee," I said, "and my name's Bryan, and I live with Mrs Webster." She just said:

"I know."

Everything I said, she said "I know," and I realised she must have been more interested than I thought.

"I'm eight," I tried again.

"I know – and so am I," she said.

Then the bell went and my first date was over. During the arithmetic class I scrawled a note:

'I like you. Will you be me girl friend?' and, boldly, I put two crosses underneath.

I got the girl in the next desk to pass it over. Betty read it, looked up, and nodded. She looked very serious, and I was just thinking that it must mean a lot to her when I heard Mrs Banks's voice.

"Bryan Breed – bring me that piece of paper you just passed to Betty Smithson."

Betty gave it to me, going red. She went even redder as the teacher read it. Mrs Banks shook her head.

"You evacuees are fast workers. You haven't been here five minutes, and you're chasing the girls."

And all the class laughed, except the other evacuees, who looked a bit disgusted. Crumbling the note into the paper basket, Mrs Banks added:

"You do not pass notes in my class, remember that. Now get on with your sums."

I thought that might have put Betty off, but I waited for her at the school gate, and, as she came out, she smiled and let me walk across the road with her.

The next afternoon, I asked her if she would come out and play after school, and she said she would see if her mother would let her. I sent David back with Brian Webster, who grumbled about it. Her mother said we could play in their garden, and when we were up the end of it, behind some tall hollyhocks, I kissed her.

"Is that the first time you've kissed with a boy?" I said.

"It might be," she said. But she would not let me do it again that time.

When I got back, Mrs Webster said:

"I hear you've gone sweet on Betty Smithson," and smiled.

I realised Brian Webster had told on me, and when we were having tea I kicked him under the table. That night being away did not seem so bad, but I still wished it had happened in London, I was still missing Mum and Dad.

Mrs Webster was good about it and asked her up to play in our garden. We would start playing there but finish up wandering over the fields, with Dave ambling along behind.

"Will you still love me when you go back to London?" Betty was obviously thinking a long way ahead.

"That might be years," I said, "and, of course, I will."

Betty even found a way for us to meet on Saturday nights. There was a dance in the church hall, and before it started they had a children's hop between half past six and half past seven. She said her mother would let her go.

"I'm not sure I'll be allowed out to that," I said.

She looked me straight in the eye:

"I might go even if you don't."

That was enough. Jennie Webster went to the grown-up dance, and I pleaded with her to go early so that she could take me to the early one. It was fixed, though I do not think Mr Webster quite approved. I found that Betty had been getting lessons from her mother and she took me round. The music came from a gramophone that kept running out:

"I've got sixpence, a jolly, jolly sixpence, I've got sixpence to last me all my life. I've twopence to spend, twopence to lend, and twopence to take home to my wife . . .", and it would get slower and slower until somebody ran over and gave it a quick wind.

But it was marvellous, jerking round close to Betty and seeing Jennie Webster grinning at me and shaking her head in mock disapproval.

It was shortly afterwards that Mrs Webster had a letter from Dad asking if he and Mum could come down and see us, and the next Saturday they got out of the village taxi outside the cottage. David ran to them and Mum threw her arms around him, but even though I wanted to do the same, being older I thought I ought to hold back in front of the Websters. They had brought toys for us and a present for Mrs Webster.

They took us into Attleborough for the pictures, and afterwards we had fish and chips and peas. On the Sunday we took them the places we knew and the birds' nests we had found. Once or twice Mum looked a bit anxious and said:

"You won't want to come back to London with all this beautiful country and space."

But we did. We would have gone back at that moment. Seeing them had brought it all back, reawakened the old longings. I would miss Betty Smithson, but that was nothing compared with being back in London.

At five o'clock that afternoon the taxi was outside again, ready to take them back. At that moment as Mum kissed and cuddled us, I wished they had not come. The pain inside was starting up again. We waved until the taxi turned the corner and we could not see Mum and Dad's faces peering out of the back window.

I wanted to cry and rushed off down to the bottom of the garden to the only creature I did not mind seeing me in tears – the goat. I buried my head in its white side and told her all about it.

David did his crying out in the open, and when I got back Jennie Webster was comforting him.

"Come on you," I said, "you're too big now to cry."

"You're a right one to talk," she said.

We could not settle at all after the visit. David was ill, and even I could not eat. It was taking David ages to get over bronchitis, and finally Mrs Webster wrote to Mum. I saw the letter open on the table before she posted it:

'The boys, especially David, are fretting. I think it would be wise for you to come and stay. We can put you up here only for a short time, but you are welcome until you can find something bigger.'

Mum and Dad came again, and this time only Dad went back on the Sunday. She had to sleep with us, and in the morning it was great seeing her between us. We sang 'Jesus bids us shine' every night and David began to get better almost at once.

Shortly afterwards, we said goodbye to the Websters. Mum found two rooms in a farmhouse belonging to some people called Fisher.

"Our two sons are away in the Forces," they said. "You're welcome to the rooms and to share the kitchen."

Mum went to work on the land to help pay the rent, and in the school holidays we went with her and learnt how to hoe sugar beet and pick potatoes and carrots. It was lovely having her with us, and for the first time we began to appreciate the country. We found birds' eggs, but only took one from each nest. We made holes in the ends and blew out the yolk so that we could keep them in a box we called our collection. Our favourites were the thrush's eggs, like a blue sky with black spots of rain.

We went fishing in the ponds with a piece of elm and a hairpin, but never caught anything. We crept up on lizards sunning themselves on the road banks, and longed to pounce on the cock pheasants which strutted almost in front of you. They somehow knew they were protected birds, said Mr Fisher, and that nobody would shoot them.

And Betty Smithson came everywhere and did not mind being kissed at any time nobody was looking. Once she even let me see her knickers, though afterwards I wondered what all the fuss was about.

We even got two rabbits given to us and we kept them in a hutch outside, learning which leaves to collect to feed them on. It came as a bit of a shock to find out that they were valuable.

"You look after them well," said Mr Fisher one day, "and old Baynard up by the chapel will give you half a crown for them."

"We won't never sell them," said David rubbing the nose of one through the wire netting.

Mum was getting excited. Christmas was three weeks away and Dad would be coming down. She told us he would come laden with presents from everybody at home, and we got excited too. It was when we were passing the village store after leaving school one day that I said to David:

"I think we ought to buy a present for Mum and Dad."

"What wiv?" He was always practical.

"I don't know yet – perhaps we can earn the money or something. Let's have a look in the shop anyway."

They had a special shelf for gifts, since not everybody could go into Attleborough for their Christmas shopping. The brooch was in the middle. It was in the shape of a bird, and its wings were made out of blue stones. I nudged David.

"I bet Mum would love that . . ."

I looked at the little ticket on it.

"But it'll cost three shillings, and if we buy Dad ten Woodbines it will mean we'll need at least four shillings."

We came out of the shop feeling fed up. Next day was Saturday and we went round the village seeing if there were any odd jobs we could do. The people seemed to think it was a bit of a cheek, and we only had twopence at the end of the day.

On Monday and Tuesday of the following week we went into the village store to make sure the brooch had not been sold. On Wednesday we asked Mr Dove, the owner, if he could put it on one side for us. We could give him twopence deposit. In the end he said he would as long as we paid for it in full by four o'clock the next Saturday afternoon, the last one before Christmas. We said we were certain to do that.

By two o'clock on the Saturday we had earned only sixpence and sat down by the road to think of what we could do. In the end I said:

"You do want Mum to have that Christmas present don't you?"

"Yes, but how?" said David.

"The rabbits. We can sell the rabbits for half a crown each."

"No – not them."

"Look – it's the only way out. Perhaps somebody will send us some money as a present and we can buy them back when Dad gets here."

David was reluctant, but allowed me to persuade him. We went back to the house and, gently as we could, put the rabbits into a sack. They did not like it and clawed around all the way.

"Will you buy our rabbits?" I said when Mr Baynard's thick glasses peered through the door.

"Let me have a feel," and his hand went inside the sack.

"They'll do," he said at last.

He took the sack and gave us two half crowns, and closed the door as if he was in a hurry. David was upset, but I cheered him up by telling him how pleased Mum would be with the brooch.

We had got about fifty yards down the road when we met Brian Webster.

"What have you two been up to?" he asked nastily, like he always did.

"We just sold our rabbits for half a crown . . ."

"You know what will happen to them don't you?" said the Webster boy grinning slyly.

"Wot?"

"He'll wring their necks and send them to London to be eaten."

"Oh, my wabbit, my wabbit," said David, and we both raced back to the house. We could get no reply at the front so we raced round to the shed at the side.

"I'm in here," called Mr Baynard. "What do you want now?"

As we got to the entrance, we saw them. They were hanging up on a rack, hooks through their legs, their necks loose. We rushed forward and felt them. They were still warm, but they were quite dead.

David did not speak to me for days, but we did buy the brooch and the Woodbines. We could not wait until Christmas and gave Mum her present next day.

"Oh, it's lovely, the loveliest I've ever had," she said. While she was cuddling us she added gently:

"This is what you did with the money from the rabbits."

I had not wanted her to know, but in Rockland things got around. Dad liked his Woodbines too, and he gave us some money to buy more rabbits with. We never did.

It was a few weeks after Christmas, whilst we were sitting in front of the fire in our pyjamas, that Mum said she had something to tell us. One of the Fisher boys had been wounded and had been invalided out of the army. Mrs Fisher needed her room again.

"We have to move from here and there is nowhere we can all go together. And your Dad says he needs me in London." Seeing our look she added quickly. "Oh, you're all right now. You've stopped fretting – and look at you. Look how big you are."

We had only stopped fretting because she was there, I thought. I also considered it a bit selfish of Dad to want Mum all to himself.

Two weeks later Mum took us down to the Smiths' house, right opposite the pub and the store in the middle of the village. Frank Smith was the village builder and decorator and people said that he and his thin, dark-haired wife could make a shilling go further than anybody else in Rockland.

They had a grown-up daughter, Rose, and a thirteen-year-old son named Bernard who was in another class at the village school. Everybody called him Patchy Smith because his trousers had more patches than trousers. They were the only people who would take us.

When the taxi drew up to take Mum to Attleborough for the train, Mrs Smith said:

"It's a pity you didn't think to go on a Wednesday, Mrs Breed. The bus comes through then and it would have saved you five shillings."

As soon as the taxi had gone that feeling returned inside and I could see from his face that David had it too. We slept in an upstairs room with Bernard, and it was lit with a candle instead of oil lamps. That first night we both wet the bed. It was the first time we had ever done it, but Mrs Smith did not believe us and refused to change the sheets.

That first morning we learnt how the Smiths got their reputation.

"We need something for a pie tonight," said Mrs Smith. "Bernard – show them how we do it."

Bernard took us down to the bottom of the garden. He propped up a heavy iron grid with a piece of wood, and put some seed underneath. Attached to the stick was a long piece of string. He took the end of this and ducked into a little shed about ten yards away, beckoning to us to follow.

"What's that for?" I asked when we were inside looking out through a little hole in the wall.

"It's a bird trap. We're going to catch birds for tonight's dinner."

"What sort of birds?" asked David.

"Any of 'em – blackbirds, thrushes, even sparrows. You're lucky if you gets a pigeon."

Then he told us to be quiet, and we waited. A blackbird was the first to be tempted by the seed. Bernard jerked the string and the grid thudded down on top of it. He raced out, grabbed the bird and pulled at its neck. A drop of red bubbled on to the yellow of its beak and it lay still.

"You cruel pig, you," said David.

"What's up with you?" said Bernard, genuinely surprised at our reaction. "You eat meat don't you?"

Despite ourselves we watched fascinated as he executed another blackbird, a sparrow and a thrush. That night Mrs Smith put a pie on the table It smelt delicious. We had had only a slice of bread for lunch, and we were hungry, but we would not eat any of the pie. We watched in horror as the Smiths picked and sucked at the tiny bones.

"You'll have to learn to like it," said Mrs Smith, "or make do with tatties and gravy."

We found that the Smiths wasted nothing. Most of the garden was used. There was not a flower to be seen, and the parts that were not heavy with vegetables were used for rearing chickens, and even ducks. They were crafty with it, too. They had an asparagus bed, but it was very rarely they ate any themselves: it went across to the shop to be sold. They bought baby chicks and ducks and fed them up for selling. The only person who ever got an egg was Mrs Smith's nephew who was an insurance collector. He called on Tuesday, always at lunch time and always singing, "I don't want to set the world on fire, I just want to light a flame in your heart", as he came up the path.

We met Mrs Fisher and her daughter in the fields one day, and she asked us how we were getting on at the Smiths. We told them about the bird pies.

"Tight as a mouse's arsehole those Smiths are," Mrs Fisher said to her daughter.

We could not tell Mum all this because Mrs Smith read our letters, but since she sent us to post them, we used to write on the flap at the back 'We want to come home'.

Either David or I were always doing things that got us sent to bed early and I think it was really to save the oil and the candles. Sometimes we also got a lick or two of the cane Mrs Smith kept for really special occasions.

Bernard's prize possession was a rusted old grown-up bike, which he guarded as if it were made of gold.

"Don't you ever ride my Bernard's bike," warned Mrs Smith. "He thinks the world of it, and it's the only plaything he's ever had to himself. If you ever do it any harm there'll be murders."

We managed to resist it at first, but one afternoon we were left on our own, and he had forgot to padlock the shed where he kept it. It was big for me but I wobbled down the village street with David sitting on the carrier. The air rushed past us, and we laughed and shouted our way out of the village on the road to Rockland St Peter's Church. I forgot about the steep hill. We gathered speed and half-way down I realised we were going too fast to get round the bend at the bottom. I applied the brakes, but too suddenly. The bike swerved, straight into the ditch full of mud. We got out, but the bike had disappeared under the slime.

"You don't half smell," said David as we climbed back up the hill.

"So do you," I said, "but that's the least of our worries."

I had never seen Mrs Smith so angry, but then she was egged on by the fit Bernard threw when we told him what had happened to his bike.

"You'll go straight to bed without any supper," she raged, "but first you'll show Mr Smith where you sunk my boy's bike."

Mr Smith would not let us into his builder's van. He said it would smell for weeks if he did. He drove down to the hill and we walked to meet him there. It was easy to see where we had gone in because where we had pulled ourselves out, the bank was still covered with mud.

Swearing at us, Mr Smith poked about in the mud with a long pole for several minutes before he found something solid. Then he poked hard again and pulled. It was the bike all right, but he had put the pole right through the spokes of the front wheel.

"It's broken, Dad," said Bernard, "the front wheel's broken."

He must have known he would have to wait for a replacement until his father happened to come across an old wheel on his travels. He would never buy a new one.

Mrs Smith made us wash down in cold water. She was not heating water just for us, she said. Later, we could hear the Smiths eating downstairs, and she told Bernard to come up and tell us what we had gone without.

As well as missing home, most of the time at the Smiths we were miserable and hungry. We began to write 'We want to come home' in even bigger letters on the back of the letters to Mum and Dad.

The only excitement came when Mrs Smith insisted her husband should take us with him when he went shooting or fishing. For him they were not hobbies, but ways of saving yet more money. He never wasted a cartridge for he never shot unless he was certain of hitting something. In fact, most of his shooting was of pigeons as we all sat waiting in hides and getting a clip round the ear if we so much as said a word.

Mr Smith was very cautious and waited until the pigeons were in the branches directly above or pecking a few feet away. It seemed cowardly. The birds did not stand a chance, but I think he was scared of wasting a cartridge.

We did not like the fishing so much. It was all right when you got there, but because Mr Smith always said there was not enough room in the van we had to walk, and the river was at least five miles away. But the fish was a change from blackberries and sparrows, and Mr Smith sometimes relaxed and talked about the war.

Most of it was about being in trenches in the mud, and how many Germans he himself had shot. I remember thinking he must have waited for them to get awfully close, if the pigeons were anything to go by . . . but perhaps he was not so careful with somebody else's bullets. There was one particular incident which gave him great pleasure, and he told this time and time again.

He was sitting in a trench all by himself one day, he said, just minding his own business when he heard a patting sound and singing. Slowly, very slowly, Mr Smith dragged out the story by dragging out the words and repeating them – he peered over the top of his trench.

"I could not believe me eyes," he always said seriously. "There was this big fat Jerry out of his trench with a spade, patting at the mound of earth in the front. It was as if he was doing his gardening, and was singing softly to himself as he worked. He must have been a mad one.

"I waited until he had his back towards me, and was bending forward doing his patting, and took aim at his great big behind. Then I let him have it. He yelled and shot forward faster than the bullet from my gun. I could hear him moaning for ages afterwards . . ."

And then Mr Smith would laugh and laugh and laugh until his eyes started to water and he had to wipe them. Sometimes he would try and repeat the story when we were sitting over one of the meagre meals, but Mrs Smith always told him to shut up because it was not right at meal times and, besides, she had heard it all before.

Betty got us invited to her house for tea as often as she could, and we must have really made pigs of ourselves.

I had been seen walking around with Betty so much now that the other evacuee kids kept asking us when we were going to get married. I still got a thrill out of walking along with my arm round her waist, or pulling her into the bushes to give her a kiss, but it was about this time that I received my first real lesson into the ways of women.

One evening two girls who were in a class one up at school were hanging around in the lane which ran alongside the Smiths' garden. They were Jane and Judy. I knew them because they lived in the Council houses when we were living with the Websters. They were grinning at us through the hedge.

"Hello," said Judy, "fancy seeing you."

I noticed that they had both borrowed some of their mother's lipstick, and there were red patches on their cheeks.

"Why don't you come out and have a walk with us?" Jean was giggling.

I was suddenly flattered. They were both at least a year older than me.

"Where to?" I said.

"Oh, nowhere in particular," said Jean.

"All right," I said, not seeing that I had anything to lose. "Come on, Dave."

"Not him – just you."

"I don't want to go," sulked David, realising he was not wanted. "And they're too big for you anyway."

As soon as I was with them in the lane they started walking quickly towards the fields at the top of it. Once there, Judy took my arm and put it round her waist.

"My turn next," laughed Jean.

I could not understand it. I seemed to have a fatal fascination for them. It must be that I had a way with women, though I had not noticed it before. By the time Jean had had her turn with my arm round her waist we were right in the middle of a field of tall hay.

As if they had agreed on an exact place, the two girls sat down and invited me to sit between them. Judy plucked a piece of hay and began tickling my leg.

"Have you ever kissed a girl with lipstick on?" she asked.

I had never kissed anybody except Betty before. Betty! What would Betty do if she knew where I was? But I felt strangely excited, and I wanted to see what would happen.

"No – why?"

"It's lovely. Why don't you find out what it's like?"

Then suddenly Judy pushed me back and she was over me and a pair of bright red lips were right in front of my eyes. Then they were down over mine and my mouth was full of the sticky, sweet taste of lipstick. I could feel Jean's hand rubbing my legs. It seemed to go on for ages and when she at last pulled back I was gasping for breath. She seemed pleased with the effect she had had.

"Now my turn," and Jean's lips came down before I had regained my breath. Suddenly I realised that this was different. She was pushing her tongue into my mouth. I began to enjoy it much more than I had with Judy, but suddenly she began to squirm and giggle. Then she rolled off and I could see that Judy had her hand up her skirt and was tickling her.

"Fuck off," said Jean. "What did you do that for?"

"You seemed to be taking it too seriously," said Judy, making a funny face. "We've got to go home now anyway."

As we were walking back, Judy said:

"Would you like to go out with us again?"

"I wouldn't mind," I said, but feeling a bit scared. Betty would never know, and I had a strange feeling I might learn something, though I could not think what it might be.

As soon as I saw Betty next morning I knew that something was wrong. All during class she would not look at me, and at playtime I had to seek her out.

"I hear you've got two new girl friends," she said.

"How did you know that?"

"They told me."

"It don't mean anything," I said.

"You do what you like – see if I care."

For the rest of the day she would not talk to me.

That evening Judy and Jean were in the lane again.

"I didn't like you telling Betty Smithson. You know I go out with her," I said.

"But you said you wanted to go out with us again," said Judy looking very serious. "We've fallen for you."

"Just come for a friendly walk up the road?" pleaded Jean.

Poor girls, they've both fallen for me. I thought I had better put them out of their misery and agreed to a friendly stroll up the village street.

They could not have timed it better. As we were going past Betty's house, she came out with her mother. She did not look at me, but her mother smiled. We were about twenty yards past them when Jean turned and yelled out:

"He's going out with me now."

"And me," laughed Judy.

I shrivelled up inside. I wanted to call out that it was not true, but I would not. We had not gone another fifty yards when Judy and Jean stopped.

"Look," said Judy, "we've changed our minds. We don't want to go out with you any more. You're a bit too young for us."

"Cheerio," said Jean. Then they turned and ran up the road, and I could hear them laughing for ages, even when they had turned the bend.

Next morning at school one of the other girls explained it to me gleefully. Jean and Judy had had a row with Betty the week before. They had only gone after me to get at Betty, and I had fallen for it. So much for my fatal fascination. I realised that I really did enjoy kissing Betty better. I told her so, but she just tossed her head and walked away. The next afternoon after school I saw her taking Kennie Drummond into her garden, and I knew that she had made sure I would see her holding hands with him as they crossed the road.

"You're a big twerp," said David watching with me. "It means we won't get invited to tea at Mrs Smithson's any more."

Two days later my indignity was complete when I saw Betty Smithson letting Kennie kiss her in the playground. She had never let me do that in such a public place. There did not seem anything to live for any more, except getting back to London.

It almost coincided with the baby duck episode. Mrs Smith had just bought another batch of baby ducks for rearing, and did nothing but moan about how expensive they were getting.

She kept them under a frame filled in with wire, but if anybody lifted it the ducks could escape. David fascinated by their fluffiness, and the way they took in water He would watch them for hours, but he would never touch them, because he was afraid of hurting them.

Bernard was fascinated too, but he liked to torment them. He would wait until they were all in the middle round the feeding bowl then lift the frame. Most of them would immediately waddle across to escape, but before they could actually get out, Bernard would drop the frame.

The second evening after the arrival of the baby ducks, Mrs Smith came rushing to the end of the garden, shouting:

"Who did it? One of my ducklings has been killed and I want to know who has done it. Into the house."

It was quite obvious she had already made up her mind who the murderer was. As we passed the pen we could see what had happened. One of the little things was laying with its neck caught under the frame, and its eyes were closed.

I knew who had done it. One of them had only failed by a neck to take the chance of escaping offered by Bernard. The Smith boy had disappeared some time before As soon as we got in the house, Mrs Smith got out her cane.

"I'll find out who did it." She banged the cane down on the table. "Even if I have to beat it out of you.

"David, you've been hanging around that pen all afternoon. You did it, didn't you?"

"No I didn't," said David, almost as angry as she was. "I wouldn't touch them, honest I wouldn't."

"He didn't do it," I said. "He's been with me all the time. I know he hasn't."

"You're a bigger liar than he is," said Mrs Smith. "He must have done it."

She gave Dave six across the backside and me one extra for telling lies. Just then Bernard came in, and when he saw what was happening he grinned.

"What's wrong then, Mother?" he said, having a job keeping a straight face.

"This one has killed one of my ducklings, and neither of them will own up."

"You just can't trust them with anything," I heard him say to his mother as we went up to bed, yet again with sore behinds and nothing in our stomachs.

Next day, I tore a piece of paper from my exercise book at school and borrowed twopence for a stamped envelope from the village store.

I told Mum that we had had enough and she had better come and take us back before we ran away.

Three days later Mrs Smith got a letter from Mum saying that London had not been bombed for a few weeks and she thought it would be safe for us to return. She would be down the following Saturday to collect us. I think the Smiths were as relieved as we were, but I thought, with a feeling of satisfaction, that they'd miss the seven-and-six a week they got as a fee for looking after us.

As the taxi moved off I said 'good riddance', but I ached a little for Betty and was sorry that I had not had the chance to say goodbye.

She might have forgiven me, and there may have been one more meeting with those sweet little lips.

Chapter VI

It was 1943, and we had been in Norfolk nearly three years. When we got home to Peabodys, Mum had a surprise for us. Instead of going into A block, she led us across the square to H block. We were in the luxury class: a flat with two bedrooms and a living room.

"It used to belong to Mrs Bishop – her that got compensation for being run over by a horse drawn fire engine when she was little," said Mum. "She copped her lot when a piece of shrapnel got her on her way 'ome from the Dog and Truck one night. Her old man never lasted six months afterwards – died of a broken heart, they say, though I believe meself falling fifty feet down that manhole in the blackout didn't 'elp all that much. Good old East End family they was. I used to go to school with their Tommy."

It was right opposite where K block used to be before the aerial torpedo got it. You looked down on the spot from our new windows.

"Do you believe in ghosts?" I said to Dave that night, remembering the arm without a body that Dad found, and wondering if the body ever came back to look for it.

Back again. The smokey smell of it, the grey grime of it, were better than all the green grass and the flowers. Stepney was a bit of a mess. There were more gaps than buildings, and over near the Tower there were the remains of huge office blocks that had been bombed and left. The debris was in such huge chunks that the kids called it 'the rocks' and it was the favourite place for playing wars. At the moment, though, it was quiet.

"Jerry got such a pasting that he can't afford no more bombers," said Mum. "Our boys gave 'em what for."

You would have thought we had won the war. Dad did not.

"It's not over yet," he warned. "We've won in the desert, and now the Yanks have come in we'll have enough soldiers, but I wouldn't be too sure Hitler's finished with us yet."

We went to a temporary school in Swan Street, right opposite Ibex House where Mum still office-cleaned. We did not learn much: the teacher spent most of her time finding out what we did and did not know. She was just beginning to sort that one out when Hitler showed he still knew where London was.

It was a shock when the air raid warning went. They were so out of practice it took everybody much more time to get down to the shelter. It was just after school hours, and this time we went into the shelter that was right alongside H block.

"It's lucky they wasn't still on their way 'ome from school," Mum said to Rose Olde, the woman who lived underneath us, with the five foot nothing husband and the two daughters.

"Wonder what it will be this time?" Rose replied. "Could be a mistake – I mean it's been so long, those Jerry pilots must have forgotten the way."

The shelter was one of those with bunks in, but it smelt damp and unused. Suddenly somebody shouted:

"Quiet – quiet everybody."

He stopped even Mrs Olde talking – something her little husband could not do. Overhead was a funny, droning noise. It was like an aeroplane flying low, but it was somehow different.

It seemed to be right above us for hours, then suddenly it stopped.

"It's a German plane coming down," said Mrs Olde. "Must be . . ."

Before she could finish there was a loud explosion. The brick walls seemed to move and the bunks rattled.

"That one was close," said Mum, her face drawn and white.

"At least they've got one down," said Mrs Olde, still thinking it was a plane.

There was a lot of chattering as people speculated about how far away it had come down. Then it started again. The same steady drone, though not so close, then the engine stopped. A few seconds later, another explosion.

"That's bleedin' funny," said Rose. "Two Jerries shot down so close . . ."

It was even funnier when it kept on happening. Aeroplane noises, the sudden silence, then the big bang. When the all clear went we left the shelter and everybody was mystified. It happened during several raids after that.

To us, it seemed days later that Mum switched on the wireless and the voice was talking about 'buzz bombs' and 'doodlebugs'. He explained that Hitler had launched a new weapon against London: planes with a bomb but without a pilot that crash landed and exploded. When the engine cut out it floated down. They called them doodlebugs because they did a lot of doodling before doing anything.

After that, it was worse. As we sat there between the nude walls of the shelter, we waited again and again for the drone, then the silence, then the explosion.

"Worse than ordinary bombs," said Rose. "At least you did not know what hit you. A direct hit and it was all over. With those bleedin' things you gets blown up in your mind three or four times before it explodes."

She was right. As soon as you heard one coming you listened for it to stop. As soon as it did, Mum would grab Dave and I to her and half cover us with herself. I could feel her holding her breath and her heart beating whilst we waited. The bang itself was really a relief.

"Some poor sods have copped it. God 'elp 'em," Mum always seemed to say. "Wonder where that one came from?"

For a time I thought that Hitler knew us all personally, and had decided when we would be blown to bits. After one had exploded, and God had been told by a voice to help its victims, somebody else always said:

"If yer name's on it, luv, there's nothing you can do to alter it."

I could see Germans in helmets, clutching brushes and tins of white paint, writing on the side of buzz bombs: "To Joe Reilly, and his wife Mary; Emmanuel Cohen and his son Jacob; Grandma Desmond, and her grandchild Tessa; and all at number 9, 10 and 11 Hessel Street." I even wondered when they had us in mind. In the end I asked Dad one night in the shelter, and he said it was just a way of accepting fate, of saying that what would happen, would happen.

The buzz bombs were a day and night happening now. We even saw one or two if we were slow in getting to the shelter. They were like a black cross in the sky with fire coming out of one end. The wireless said that our pilots and ack-ack gunners were shooting a lot down before they got to London.

"They must be missing a hell of a lot, too," said Rose, "judging by the bombed sites I've seen. It's getting so bad they'll soon be bombing holes."

For a while, we used to go to bed, hoping that Hitler would give it a miss for one night, but the mad cry of the siren would always disturb our dreams. Then we started going down to the shelter in our pyjamas and sleeping in the bunks. It was when the buzz bombs destroyed a dock wall and a factory at the bottom of the turning that Dad decided that Hitler was getting our range.

"If you blew hard on that shelter it might fall down," he said. "A lot of people are going down the tubes to sleep. You could have a direct hit right above your head there and not feel a thing. But you have to get down there early to get a place."

So that night, carrying bundles of blankets tied up with string, we trundled up Leman Street – which everybody called Lem*o*n Street – towards Aldgate East tube station. It was just two stops before we got out: Mark Lane, then out at the Monument. From there, it was a short trip down a long flight of moving stairs to the platform of the Bank station.

Our bedroom was a tubular cave, or rather the couple of yards nearest the wall farthest away from the trains. They had put a spider's web of connecting bunks along the wall, but people were allowed to make one more bed on the stone floor in front of each set of bunks on the platform.

Some people had risked leaving their bedding on the bunks to reserve their places, but there were gaps. As soon as Dad saw three empty ones, he stopped.

"This will do." Then to Mum. "We don't want to go too far from the escalator just in case."

It was only after being down the tube for some nights that I learnt what the 'in case' was. The Bank was nearly the deepest underground station in London, but it was very near the river. If there was the right kind of explosion it was possible that the water could come flooding up the tube into the station. After I heard about it, I told Dad I was worried because I could not swim.

"I can't either," he laughed. "Look, there is nothing to worry about. When the last train goes through they put flood gates across the hole, so nothing can happen after that."

He did not say anything about the time before the gates went across. There was very little sleeping for any of us those first few nights. Mum tried to put us to bed early, but every few minutes there was a rumbling sound which would get louder and louder until a red train roared into the station. Then it would be the clatter, clatter of shoes on the stone, the 'mind the doors, please', the slither as the doors came together, and the train whining its way back into the tube.

In the end Mum did what all the other Mums did: let us play around until the last train had gone through at just after midnight and then try to get to sleep at the same time as everybody else. At first it was hard to sleep, and you gazed up at the brick-shaped white tiles, wondering when all this was going to end and you could sleep in a proper bed again. But after a while you got used to it and sleep came almost instantly. The alarm clock was the rumbling of the first train at half past five.

It was always warm and smelly down there. When we came out of Aldgate East Station in the dawn, the air smelt so sweet it was almost sickly. The trouble with going down the tube was that we never knew what we would find when we got home.

"One of these days," Mum said several times, "we'll get down John Fisher Street and find just a hole instead of H block."

"At least you won't be in it," said Dad.

Some mornings it was obvious that a lot of doodlebugs had got through. There was smoke, and there were new gaps along our way home, and then Mum would always walk faster to know the worst quicker. The tall grey block was always there, a few more pock marks on its face, caused by the shrapnel, and a window or two missing, but just as solid as ever.

I did not like going down the tube at first, but after Mum let us roam a bit it was about the best funfair we had ever been to, and there were lots of perks.

Little gangs of us would ride between stops, trying to run up the down escalators, and explore the passages which connected with the other lines. The perks came from blokes in swanky brown uniforms who talked funny.

"Got any gum, chum?" We learnt to say as we barred their way up a passage. Most of the American soldiers obliged. They got an issue of chewing gum, and they knew that we were having trouble with sweet rationing. We sometimes saw grown-ups, especially the single girls, asking them for camels. We were a bit puzzled by this until we saw that Camels were an American fag.

One of the best games was helping the tea lady on and off the tube at different stops. She had a trolley with two big tea urns on it and some cakes. At first it used to be a tease, with us spilling more tea than she sold, but after she started bribing us with the odd cake we played it straight.

It was a lark at first, but after a few weeks everybody looked bad. Even David had puffy bags in the middle of his face under his eyes. Mum and Dad began to look ill. It was only getting five hours sleep a night that did it. They were still working and we were still going to Swan Street school.

Several times I fell asleep over my desk top and the teacher shook me to wake me up. There was no rest, even during the day. The siren went often, and we seemed to spend more time under the school in the shelter than at lessons. I began to get worried. Not about the buzz bombs or the black circles under all our eyes, but about a familiar feeling which was growing inside me. I could feel that atmosphere again, like it had been the last two times. At first,

Mum had convinced herself that the doodlebugs would not last long.

"It must be expensive for 'im wasting all them aeroplanes," she said. "That swine won't be able to keep it up."

She still thought of doodlebugs as being planes without the man in them. She got gradually more worried as the time went by and the bugs kept coming, day and night. The going down the tube had been a kind of last resort.

It was while we were having tea one night just before we left for our beds on the Bank station that Mum said to Dad:

"Well, I've done it. They go on Thursday from Christian Street school."

"Good – I think it's the right thing to do," was all that Dad said.

"What's going on Thursday?" I chipped in, though from the sinking feeling, I knew the answer. Mum did not look at us, but kept her eyes down cutting doorsteps of bread.

"You and David," she said. "They shouldn't 'ave kept on sending the doodlebugs, then you wouldn't have to go away again."

"But we're safe enough down on the tube," I protested.

"It can't be doing you no good," said Dad, "getting no sleep. You need to be away from it all so that you can get some schooling in peace as well. You've had no regular learning since you came back from Norfolk. That's what concerns me . . ."

"Dad, we don't care," David said. "We want to stay 'ome. We don't like being away . . ."

Dad seemed to lose his temper, though I could see it was a way of shutting us up:

"Just be quiet . . . you're going. And that's that. Now go and get ready for the tube."

"No, I'm not going . . . you can't make me," I shouted. "I'll run away . . ."

Without thinking I ran out through the door. Mum called down the stairs as I jumped them several at a time, but when I reached the square I did not know what to do. It was the blackout and it was dark. Finally I went and hid round D block, shivering now, to see what would happen. After a while Dad's face peered round H block entrance, but he could not see me.

About a quarter of an hour later Mum, Dad and David came out carrying the tube blankets. I ran round D block and watched them go out through the square into John Fisher Street. They had not even bothered to look, I thought, annoyed. They might at least have called out before going to the tube without me. It was July but I felt cold. What would I do when the sirens went? I wished now that I had waited and chosen daylight to run away in. At least they would have missed me at school.

In the end I decided that if the siren went I would go into a shelter where they would not know me, and I hurried out of the square through the back way, under the dark railway arches, into Katherine Street. There were old blocks of flats there and they all had shelters.

I stood on the corner by a lamp post which showed no light, and waited for the siren to go. Nobody went out in the blackout unless they had to, and the street was deserted. Several times I wanted to tear off up Leman Street to the brightness and closeness of the Bank station, but I fought off the temptation. They had to be made to realise that I meant it, to be made to feel sorry for sending us away again. I had just decided that Mum and Dad could not really love us, otherwise they would not do it, when a hand grabbed me by the collar and another hand clipped my ear.

For a moment I thought it might be a German parachutist, but when my terrified face looked up it was Dad. He began to haul me up the road towards Leman Street.

"You dare ever do anything like that again," was all he said all the way to the Bank.

I tried to look upset about being caught, but I was glad really. When we reached our place on the platform, a woman in the next bunk said:

"What's all this about running away? You mustn't go worrying yer muvver like that. They're only trying to do their best by yer, yer know."

"You mind yer own business," I said and ran off down the platform to find an American with some gum.

The day after next Mum woke us early. There was the same complete change of underwear, the same little case with our few things in, the same dismal walk, but this time up Cable Street to Christian Street, where all the Jews lived. Just to be awkward, Mum said.

She was crying again when she left us. Don't know why she sends us away if it upsets her so much. Once she had gone we soon realised we were evacuees again. People asking us questions, ordering us about and marching us along in twos. I was eleven now, and I had to look hardened, an experienced evacuee who knew what it was all about. As soon as the bus we were in turned up Commercial Street, I said knowingly:

"Bloody Liverpool Street again."

"They ain't sending us back to that Mrs Smiff again are they?" said David.

"She wouldn't 'ave us," I said, hoping I was right, but dreading the thought.

Even the train looked the same. Kids hanging out of windows and shouting rude things and laughing at the new arrivals. I could not join in. I was fed-up with it all. When would they stop making us go away? When would they hang Hitler on the Siegfried Line? When Dad had said goodbye he had added that we were winning the war and it would soon be over. People kept on saying that but the buzz bombs kept on coming.

The train had only got to the outskirts of London when the siren went, and the train stopped. A man came round and told us all to get on the floor away from the windows, already gummed up with tape to keep them from shattering into too many pieces. There were quite a lot of explosions, but they were a long way off, and most of the noise came from a little boy who kept on moaning in a loud voice about wanting a pee.

When there had not been a bang for a long time, the all clear went and the train started moving again. It was the usual slow stop-start journey, and we were right out of sandwiches by the time we stopped at a station for the first time and a lot of the kids got off.

I called out to a bloke in a uniform on the platform.

"Where's this then, cock?"

"It be St Ives," he said in a funny voice.

"Where's that? Never 'eard of it."

"It be in Cambridgeshire."

At least it wasn't Norfolk, I thought. After that we kept stopping at every little station and a few kids bawled out at each one. We got turfed out at a place called Wisbech.

"Wonder who we'll get this time," said David as we filed on to an old bus outside the station. As usual, we did not stay in the town, and the bus coughed its way out into the country. We stopped outside the usual church hall – corrugated iron painted grass colour, like the inevitable W.V.S. ladies waiting inside.

"Lou Bates of Maltmas wants two boys," said one of them ushering David and me outside and into her little car – green, of course.

She chatted away as we drove through the village, round the clock tower right in the middle, and down a long turning. Then she turned into a gate and a track surrounded by barns and stables. Just a few yards on was a house with a garden in front. Immediately the car stopped, a brown dog came wagging towards us, and jumped up to lick our faces.

"He's luvly," said David, laughing for the first time since we left Peabody's. "Does 'e live 'ere?"

"She . . . it's a she, boi," boomed a voice.

We looked up to see a big, round woman, with red apples for cheeks, coming down the path.

"These is my two, then," she said to the woman who had brought us. Then, to us:

"I expects you could do with somethin' inside you . . . Flossie, down girl, down."

And she led the way up the path to the house, Flossie following, quieter now, behind us.

Immediately we stepped inside our eyes were magnetised to the huge table in the middle of the even huger room. On it was a big bowl piled high with strawberries and beside it was a glass bowl of cream. And spread round them were an apple pie, a cold rice pudding, a flan with big chunks of fruit in it, and a currant cake.

When we came out of the spell of it all, and our eyes reluctantly roamed from the table, she was standing with her arms crossed just looking at us, her eyes smiling, obviously enjoying our reaction. It did not take us long to realise that if you wanted to please Lou Bates, or Aunt Lou as we were instructed to call her, you enjoyed your food and always did your best to ask for second helpings.

"You've come on a good day," she laughed. "It's my baking day . . . though I didn't make the strawberries and cream. They're from off our own holdings. We've just the one cow, but she don't do too bad. Now sit you down and eat as best you can."

She helped us to the strawberries and cream first. When she had disappeared to fetch us mugs of milk, David said, mouth full:

"This one don't seem too bad. Better than the Smiffs any day."

"You just can't see furver than yer belly," I said cruelly, thinking him a bit of a traitor to even imagine that anywhere could be as good as Peabodys, but at the first mouthful even I had forgotten for a moment that we were miles from home again.

Then there was apple pie, and she insisted on putting the rice pudding with it. We had never had them together before, but it was lovely. We could hardly fit in the cake, but we did. David sat back and groaned:

"Oh my belly . . . it's so full I can hardly move."

Aunt Lou chuckled so hard that the whole of her seemed to move. It was only after things had been cleared away and Aunt Lou was in the outhouse washing up under the pump, that there was time to see where we were. The table was the centrepiece of the low ceilinged farmhouse kitchen. It was set on highly polished red bricks, as were two big armchairs, either side of a wide coal fire with two ovens alongside it. Although it was a warm July day, the remains of a fire were still glowing in the grate.

There were two grandfather clocks along one wall, and on the other, just beside the door, a dartboard surrounded by a board so that any misses did not mark the cool cream walls.

"You 'ad better have a look round, we don't want you to get lost," said Aunt Lou when she came in from the outhouse wiping her hands on her apron.

She first took us through a door at the far end of the room. There were three stone steps going down, a level bit, and then three more steps going up to another door opposite. Before we had a chance to go up the steps Aunt Lou turned left through yet another door. It was a little room, bare bricked, with shelf upon shelf climbing to the ceiling She smiled as she watched us gaping.

Each shelf was paining under the weight of jars of fruit and vegetables, preserved eggs and small sacks of flour, and potatoes. Hanging from the ceiling were big pieces of bacon and ham. On the floor were wide pans of milk, the cream on top forming a surface you imagined you could skate on, and bowls of eggs.

"This is my larder," said Aunt Lou when she thought we had done the vision justice. "It be the coolest place in the 'owse. Don't think we'm fiddling the rationing or somethin'. All of it's off our own land. We killed a pig only last week and we're allowed to keep some of it salted as long as we has our bacon ration stopped for a time. We have a few 'ens, and we makes our own butter from the milk the cow gives. I'll let you make some butter for me tomorrow."

She did not take us up the steps to the door in front. She just pointed to it and said:

"That be my best room."

We soon learnt that nobody was allowed in the best room except on very special occasions. She took us back into the kitchen, and through another door on the same side as the grandfather clocks.

"These are the wooden stairs to Bedfordshire," she laughed.

We did not know what she meant until we scrambled up the narrow stairway after her and found ourselves in a little bedroom.

"This un's where my Ron and Ludo sleeps. We sleep in the next room, and you'll be 'aving the one at the end."

The bedrooms were arranged so that we had to go through everybody else's to get to ours at the end. Every room had an oil lamp. There was no gas, electricity or running water – apart from the pump in the outhouse. Afterwards Aunt Lou took us round the stables and we stroked the smooth greyness and the brownness of the horses.

"If you comes out here," she said, "you must always be sure to close the gates behind you. They don't all belong to us – all the smallholders keep their horses here.

"We've got about thirty acres of holdings, but there are hundreds of acres and a lot of the other smallholders is entitled to use these buildings."

We gradually got the picture from Aunt Lou's friendly and agile tongue. Everybody rented land from the Council. It wasn't all together, but in lots of thin strips, all in different places. Maltmas Farm, as Lou's place was called, was where the smallholdings started, and they stretched for mile after mile from there.

Later they all came home, their boots clattering the red brick path to the door: Jim, who was Lou's husband, Ron, who was their son, and Ludo, the evacuee with the cross eyes who had grown up to at least sixteen and stayed on the land instead of going back to London.

In many ways he became our tongue. Often you could not think of anything to say when they took the micky out of Londoners, or evacuees, and when he scored it made up for all the times you could not think of anything to say.

Uncle Jim was a small, five-foot-nothing of a man, whose big boots seemed to take up half his length, but he was well-liked and respected in the village.

"You can always rely on Jim Bates," people would say. "He'll never let you'm down when you'm needs a bit of equipment or the loan of an 'orse."

He smoked 'Digger Flake' from a huge pipe, and you often could not see the top half of him for the cloud. Later, in the emergency of Jim running out of baccy, I was often sent off on Ludo's bike to the pub for one of the square yellow packages.

Ron was taller than Ludo, though he was the same age. He had red cheeks and black hair, curling here and there, like his mother. Ron did not talk as much as Ludo, but he smiled and laughed a lot and they were very good friends. I think that was why Aunt Lou kept him on.

"What a bleedin' place to come from," grinned Ludo when we told him we lived in Stepney. "They're all fieves and rogues. You can never leave anyfing laying about."

He did not really mean it, you could tell, but you felt you had to say something.

"I thought all the people from Limehouse had slit eyes," I said. "You must be the only one from there who ain't a Chinaman."

His grin had just started to broaden when Aunt Lou called.

"You mustn't miss this," he said as he rushed towards the door. "You won't 'ave seen or tasted anyfing like this in Stepney where they don't know any better than to eat jellied eels. Lou's grub is marvellous. They say in the village that she sets the best table in Fridaybridge."

It was obviously something he had heard somebody say. Inside, Aunt Lou had built up the fire again and when we were all sitting down ready – and never before – she took a cloth and dug into the oven, her large behind coming up like a full moon. When she was upright again she was holding a baking tray upon which was a fluffy mountain of Yorkshire pudding, which still seemed to be rising as she placed it on the table. Even Uncle Jim and Ron, who must have seen such a sight many times before, could not take their eyes from it.

Already on the table was a bowl of steaming brown gravy, and as Aunt Lou cut the Yorkshire pudding into huge squares and put it on to plates, she smothered each piece with it.

As she handed Jim his plate, she said:

"You get that down you, boi, and you'll not come to much 'arm."

"That I won't, woman, that I won't," muttered Jim, his knife and fork already working.

She gave us smaller pieces, because, she explained, it might be too much after having had tea. But her idea of small was different to anybody else's we had ever come across, and it seemed to cover most of the plate. It was delicious, better than anything I had ever tasted before, soft in the middle, crisp round the edges. I looked across at David, and his eyes seemed as big as half-crowns as he gazed down at his plate. It was a funny kind of dinner, I thought, but it was nice, and I finished my bit with very little room to spare.

By that time Aunt Lou was already bustling round again. A dish of creamy white potatoes appeared and a piece of boiled ham like the side of a hill. I said I could not eat any and Aunt Lou seemed a bit disappointed. David tried a little, but failed badly. The others seemed to have no trouble at all, and the plates cleared rapidly.

Afterwards a fresh apple pie and rice pudding appeared, but Lou asked Ludo if he would prefer strawberries and they came out again with the bowl of cream.

Then, without a word, Jim, Ron and Ludo got up from the table and groaned into the armchairs round the stove, as if each knew exactly which chair was his. Aunt Lou lit the oil lamp which hung over the middle of the table, and regarded the contented results of her labours with some satisfaction. Jim got out his pipe, and Ron gave Ludo one of his packet of five Park Drives before lighting up himself. But Aunt Lou still had one other duty to perform before the washing up. She produced a brown teapot. First four teaspoons of tea, then out came a jar, and she took half a teaspoonful of the white powder in it and sprinkled it in with the tea. When she saw me staring at the jar she said:

"Crussom salts, boi, we always put a pinch in with the tea. Thems good for you."

Then, to Ron:

"The books came down this morning from May's."

May was a relative in the village. She had the books for half the week, Aunt Lou the other half, and they shared the bill.

Out came the *Farmer's Weekly*, *The Illustrated Picture Post*, *The Dandy*, and the *Beano*. After they had been reading for a time, I noticed something strange. The boys were reading the *Farmer's Weekly* and the grown-up papers. It was the *Dandy* Uncle Jim had in front of his face, scanning the pictures as he puffed away. Every so often he would chuckle, and Ron and Ludo would look at each other and grin.

It all seemed a bit strange until we found out something later that Uncle Jim had never learnt to read. Aunt Lou did all his reading for him, and filled in the forms she kept getting from some people she swore about called the Ministry of Agriculture. He relied on her completely for all the book reading and the writing, as he called it. She didn't mind. She loved being in the centre, controlling it all, and doing it beamingly and lovingly.

That night in the big bed David asked me what I thought this time. I said I would sooner be home, but remembering the strawberries and the Yorkshire pudding, it did not seem as bad as some places they had sent us to. It was strange. We were ten and eleven now, but there was still that ache inside because you needed your mother and the things you knew and trusted.

Next morning Lou came in very early.

"We're all picking today out at Laddis. You'll like that to be sure."

Breakfast was hurried. Plenty of porridge, white bread, home made jam and butter, and great mugs of hot, sweet tea. Aunt Lou said there was no time for a 'cooked breakfast' on a working day. But on the first Sunday I realised that they made up for it with porridge, and as many eggs and crinkling rashers of bacon as they could eat.

That morning, all the time we were eating, Aunt Lou was busy pushing bottles of cold, golden tea, cheese, sandwiches and bread into the shoulder bags in which each carried his own lunch before pedalling away. I went on the seat on the back of Lou's bike. David went in the same fashion with Jim, with Flossie, the dog, trotting along behind.

We wobbled up into the village, through it, and then out the other side. All the time we passed other people on bicycles, and not one passed without a word:

"Mornin' Jim, Lou. I sees your second crop is a comin' on well."

"Mornin' Lou – don't forget the whist drive on Saturday."

"Careful there, Jim boi – you'll stretch your legs carryin' all that weight."

Then we went up a path by a field and stopped alongside rows, that stretched away into the distance, of little plants with shiny leaves. Peeping through the leaves was redness. Up some of the rows there were already behinds pumping up and down.

"This is where the strawberries come from," said Aunt Lou. "We're just picking the second crop. You can help."

She handed us each a little basket she called a chip.

"We'll pay you a penny for every chip you fill up. Don't squash 'em too hard as you pull 'em off. They mustn't be damaged or the wholesaler won't take 'em. Pick the big ripe ones, but leave the little 'uns."

Then, with a laugh:

"Oh, and you can eat as many as you like as you go along. Them's part of the perks."

David looked at me as if he could not believe he was in a real world, and then dashed towards a row where nobody was already picking. I started into the row alongside him. It then became a game of one for the basket, one for me. I had filled one basket and started on another about half-way up the row when I heard David groan and saw him rolling along between the rows to disappear behind the little hut where they kept the baskets and tools.

He appeared again two minutes later wiping his mouth on the back of his hand and looking very white. I had just started to laugh when my own stomach began to ache and roll and pitch. I made for the hut even faster than he did.

When I came round it seemed as if everybody had stopped working and was looking at me. Their laughter must have been heard in the village, a good mile away.

After that every strawberry went into the chip, and at the end of the week both of us had earned a fortune: David thirteen shillings and threepence and me fifteen and six. Unfortunately, we had arrived right at the end of the strawberry picking season.

"Wished we had come sooner," said David thinking of his thirteen shillings.

"You speak for yourself," I said, still feeling homesick.

In the evening before supper we spent most of our time tumbling off sacks in the barns, making rude noises at the pigs, helping to give fresh straw to the horses. One night when we were playing in the barn nearest the road we heard voices, and looked out. Two girls were sitting on the gate the other side of the road. One was tall and dark and wearing trousers; the other was fair in an old-looking flowered dress that was too big for her.

When they saw us they started whispering and then laughing behind their hands. As if we could not see them. We had not talked to any other kids yet, and I started to walk towards them, curious to know what the locals were like, especially the local girls. They looked away, grinning, when we reached the gate, but when we pretended to walk past without noticing them, one of them whistled.

We turned round and the dark one said:

"Too stuck up to talk then, are yer? Just because you comes from London."

"It's not that," I said, "you was laughing so much I didn't fink you 'ad the time."

"Well, we 'ave," said the fair one and giggled.

The dark one turned out to be Sue Donald, who lived with her parents across one field from Maltmas Farm. The blonde was Dora Bates, a relative of Aunt Lou's who came from one of the four Council houses about half-way up Maltmas Drive. In fact, most people in the village seemed to be called Bates and were related in one way or another.

It did not take long to get friendly, and we went for a walk with them up the path that ran between the smallholdings and the Co-op orchard on the other side. I soon discovered they had some funny ideas about boys from London, and started to feel much more confident.

"We've heard all about 'ow girls aren't safe with you, and all that," said Dora, bending down to pull up a dandelion, looking sideways to see if I had noticed her showing her knickers as she did so.

"Yes," said Sue, giving Dora a shove so that she fell over, " 'ow you know what it's all about and all that."

Not safe? All about what? We knew a bit about nature's way with rabbits and cows and things, but we were not too sure about humans, though we knew that something was going on we ought to know about. I just grinned, hoping they could not tell that I did not really know what they were on about.

When we had got that over, it became quite friendly, and they began to tell us about the village. After the holiday I would be going to school with them in the school near the clock tower because I was the same age. David would have to go to the little school, across the road from the big school, until he was eleven. David said he did not think much of that. The teachers were all right, and nobody ever got the cane.

After the harvest there would be whist drives and dances in the village hall again, and everybody went to them. Sue said Aunt Lou would be bound to let us go because she always went herself, and it was sort of understood straight away that me and Sue would meet once we got there. It was like that. Sue and me liked each other from that first walk alongside the Co-op orchard.

Most nights after that Sue and Dora came down the road or we would go a little way up and wait for them. Sometimes they had another girl with them called Ida, who came from right in the middle of Fridaybridge.

After a while I started to call Sue Dick like everybody else did, but I did not really want to. To me she was very much a girl, and I did not like the idea of the boy's name.

It was at this time that Ludo and Ron came in very useful. One day when one of the pigs had just produced a litter and we were watching them sucking and squealing at the tits of the sow, I said:

" 'ow did them little 'uns get inside the sow anyway?"

"She went wiv a man pig, you twerp," he said, grinning at Ron.

I knew that there was a man pig in it somewhere from our Norfolk days, but I wanted to get him talking about it.

"You mean they just touched each other?" I asked innocently.

"You could say that," he said, again looking at Ron and laughing. "Look – he puts cock up 'er, if yer really wants to know."

"Is it the same for us?" I asked.

"You cheeky little bugger you," grinned Ludo, and I thought for a moment he was not going to let on, but then he added: "Yeh, it is. You didn't really come from under a gooseberry bush, yer know."

From then we kept on at Ludo whenever there were not any grown-ups about. We asked him if he had ever done it.

"A few times," he said with a wink.

After that it did not take long to get him boasting about it. Ron never said much, but I had the feeling he did not believe half Ludo said, especially that bit about getting two girls down at once on the way back from London.

About the same time, school started again, and every morning David and me would dawdle the mile of Maltmas Drive. We always carried a tin box layered with sandwiches, sometimes tatty, sometimes egg, sometimes cheese and sometimes, if another pig had met its end, boiled ham. At the top of the road David would carry on to the little school and I would turn in past the almond tree at the school gate.

I did not mind going. Dick, Ida and Dora were in the same class and there was a chance to chat them up at dinner time. The teacher was all right too. She was a Mrs Gottabed – which made everybody laugh to start with – who came from March, about seven miles away, in an old motor car that sometimes made her late. Her big thing was lettering. She bought pots of colour which had 'Poster Paint' written on the outside, and made us try and do posters. I thought it was a bit cissy at first, but when she began to praise some of my lettering I changed my mind. I became her star pupil when, after a lesson on Dr Livingstone, I produced a drawing of a very darkest Africa with a searchlight going right across it and the letters: 'Livingstone – searchlight on Africa'. She was so pleased she took it to show the headmistress and then put it up on the main notice board in the corridor where everybody could see it.

There were a few other evacuees in the school, but we did not need to gang up. The local kids were very tolerant, and almost regarded us with respect.

I only needed to fight once, and that was over Dick. This kid called Colin Hayward, who sat in the next desk to her, kept writing her notes and tryin to hold her hand. I did not think that Dick was doing enough to discourage him and I regarded her as my girl, even though nothing had really been said. In the end I had to show him what for, as my Mum would say. Even then I did not make it obvious it was over Dick, and I was a bit sneaky about it. The big game in the playground was rounders. One lunch time Colin was just in when I threw the ball at the corner stump and hit it.

"Out," I shouted.

"I was in," he protested.

"You want to argue about it?" I said, not giving him a chance to say no as I flew at him, fists up. He made a good fight of it. I made his nose bleed after about a minute, but he did not start crying, and he caught me a beauty in the eye. My only worry was that it made my eyes water and I did not want anybody to think I was crying. We had just got down to ground level, rolling about on the concrete, when somebody went to the teacher's room and Mrs Gottabed came out.

She made us shake hands and took us in to wash away the blood. I found out afterwards that the teachers decided that Colin Hayward must have been picking on the evacuees and I had decided to straighten him out. Colin himself knew what it was really about, and he did not bother Dick again. She knew, too. She pretended to be upset with me for starting a fight, but I thought she was quite pleased really.

I went home with a purple eye. Aunt Lou told me off for fighting and Ludo took the micky, saying he would be able to see me coming in the dark. But it was baking day and there was Yorkshire pudding – always dished up before the meal with gravy – so I did not mind.

We were still amazed at the food, and the variety of it. Pies, roasts, jams and flans squelching in fruit and cream that had only been in the cow that morning. We began to fill out, David more than me. He had always been rounded, and it was Ludo who started calling him 'Tubby', and then everybody started. He did not like it much, and swore if I called him it, though he put up with it from everybody else.

It was harvesting time when Ludo's advice about women began to produce action. I would have liked to have got Dick alone, but every evening she turned up with either Ida or Dora, or both. I told them about Ludo, the pigs, and the girls on the train, and they whispered among themselves and giggled.

"You're all talk," I kept on saying.

I would chase Dick, get her down and tickle her. She liked that, but it seemed to be getting me nowhere.

The evenings were long. Whilst the harvesting was going on and there was fine weather Jim, Ron and Ludo stayed out in the fields until dark reaping, and Lou would not put up supper until they came in. David and me were fascinated by the harvesting, not so much by the actual cutting, but by the chase for rabbits that went with it. The reaper would go round and round, the remnant of corn getting smaller and smaller. If there were any rabbits in it, they retreated farther and farther into the middle. Men would be standing around with dogs on leads, waiting for one of the rabbits to run for it. It was cruel really, and David, probably remembering the Norfolk rabbits, said so.

Sometimes he would laugh, because there were no rabbits and all that would come bustling out would be two or three tiny field mice, almost hidden by the stubble. Most times, though, there would be a rustling in the remaining corn square and a rabbit, or even a hare, would come jumping out through the stubble to try and make its escape. I never saw one make it. The dogs would be unleashed and at least one of them would make the kill, and bring the floppy brown back to its master.

It was on one of these evenings when everybody was preoccupied by the shaving of corn fields, with the sun as gold as the grain, that we were talking to Dick, Ida and Dora in the field next to Jim's cowshed. Ludo had been on about a girl he had met at a dance in Wisbech on his Saturday night out with Ron. He always went with Ron on his motorbike but this Saturday he had had to walk the three miles back because he had stayed on with the girl.

"It was worth every inch of the walk," he winked. "She knew what it was for, I can tell yer."

He claimed he had made his conquest on a flat gravestone in a churchyard.

"It was a bit cold for 'er," he grinned, "but by that time she was not caring."

The girls giggled when I told them, and said how awful that Ludo was, but they could not stop talking about it. When I found some excuse to chase Dick – I think she had pushed some straw up my trouser leg when I was pretending not to be looking – I brought her down, and whispered as I tickled:

"Shame we ain't got no gravestones handy."

"It don't 'ave to be on a gravestone," I heard her say.

When I looked at her face she was still laughing but I could see she was serious. I suddenly wanted to get up and run, but I heard myself saying:

"No, it can be anywhere – even a cowshed. Like to try?"

"If the others will, I will."

I felt myself going red as I pulled her up from the ground and towards David and the girls, who had been watching a few yards off.

"Dick says that she's willing – if you are," I shouted.

The other girls knew what I meant. Dick took them out of our hearing, and there were whispers and giggles.

At last, they stopped and came back.

"Only if we all do it together," said Dick, naming the terms.

"We don't mind," I said, assuming David was interested, though when we actually got to the cowshed I could see he had more doubts about what to do than I had.

The cows were on one side, in an enclosure, and there was a space for the straw used for their bedding. I went towards it and the others followed. Then the girls just froze, looking at each other. I did not know whether to help them, or leave it all to them. I looked at Dick, and she responded.

"Let's make up a story," Dick said. "You pretend you're American airmen who have come to stay for the night."

She was only eleven but she had heard all about American airmen. Then, with the whole of East Anglia taken over by American bases, everybody knew all about American airmen.

Now it came at last I was shyer than they were . . . but what could you do now they were all waiting? But I grinned cockily, and said:

"Well, who's first?"

They looked at each other knowingly. By the way they acted it was obvious that the first two would be Dick and Ida. Almost without thinking, I turned towards Dick. I did not want it to be Ida. Her breath smelt badly. We had all been playing round the clock tower in the centre of the village one dinner break at school. Being a Londoner, and thus a dare-devil with nothing to lose, they had dared me to kiss her. So I grabbed hold of her and did. She did not struggle. She liked it, but at the crucial childish moment her lips parted and I kissed her teeth. And her breath smelt.

They were all watching us now, and it had gone very quiet. I suddenly felt very conscious of the fact that Dick's parents were just across the field and could see the cow shed, and of the cows chewing away behind me.

I pulled my courage together and started to fumble with my short trousers and the girls began to giggle again. Then something strange happened. There were some sniggers as well . . . boys' sniggers.

The girls stopped laughing, churned in the straw, trying to hoist up their thick knickers. They took in large amounts of straw in the process, and it must have been painful.

At almost the same moment two red heads appeared in the hole at the side of the shed. It was two boys from school, brothers, who lived in the same Council houses as Dora, one of the girls at that moment pulling her dress down. The biggest Miller had gaps in his teeth which made him lisp and splutter and look stupid. Now his head was grinning through the the hole knowingly.

"I know what you was doing," he said, as if it were quite an accomplishment.

The girls were changing all colours like traffic lights. Ida always blushed and she had gone post office red. Dora had gone whiter than white. Dick, perhaps because of her dark complexion, seemed the least worried. Miller's little brother, no more than six, could not have known what we was doing, but he laughed as though enjoying the surprise.

I did not know how I should react. Somehow I felt proud that there had been somebody to witness the first conquest. Well, almost a conquest except for the actual thing. I was willing to bet that the biggest Miller had never seen a girl with her knickers off before. On the other hand, I did not want it to get out to my evacuee parents, and everybody knew that Miller, despite the missing teeth, had the biggest mouth in the village. I hoped he would not talk to any adults.

I suppose, really, I was pleased to see those carrot-topped heads. I only had vague idea notions of what I was supposed to do with Dick. She was obviously expecting it for the first time, and I did not know as much as they thought I did.

We stood there, not knowing what to do. Ida had half her skirt still caught in her black knickers. Then the grins and giggles started again, but nervously. Miller solved the problem of what to say:

"Caught you at it, didn't I?" He spluttered a fine spray into the cow shed. Then he ran laughing away across the field, a smaller version of him struggling along behind through the thick, uneven grass.

The girls were still embarrassed despite the fresh giggles. They, too, were obviously wondering who Miller would tell.

"Let's go somewhere else," I suggested, still trying to act out the bold knowing evacuee.

"Fuck off," said Ida. Dick hesitated a bit, but on the whole Ida's summary on the situation won the day, even though she still had her skirt stuck in her knickers. The three of them went out through the cow shed door with as much dignity as the shock would allow.

David and I hustled across the field to the stables where Ron, the son of the household, and cross-eyed Ludo were putting the horses in for the night. We blurted out part of the story, just to impress them.

"Dick lets you . . . and so do Ida and Dora," I said boastfully.

"How do you know?" asked Ludo craftily, looking down in judgement as he sat at the top of the gate into the stables.

"We've been on them," I said, wondering how far I dared stray from the truth, but also knowing that neither Ron or Ludo would say anything to Lou and Jim.

"How long for?" said Ron, obviously not believing us.

That was a hard one. How long were you expected to stay on top for?

"About half an hour," I said hopefully.

Ludo laughed, looking us up and down, his cross-eyes running over the woolly pull-overs we were always forced to wear, down the short trousers to the long grey socks and wellington boots.

"I can't hold back for longer than five minutes meself," he said. We did not understand. Hold what back for five minutes? He knew something about girls we did not, and we could not comment. Then he laughed again under his cloth cap, always worn at an angle:

"You want to watch you don't get the pox. Otherwise it'll drop off."

Despite the fact that we did not understand everything he said, we were beginning to feel pleased. There was a new look in Ludo's eyes.

"You buggers, you," he grinned. From Ludo that was some sort of praise . . .

At school next morning Dick was a bit funny. She would not look at me. Miller was whispering and spitting over everybody in his excitement of telling everybody what he had seen in the cowshed. She did not say much to me at dinner time. She spent most of it talking with Ida and Dora. It was obvious what they were talking about, and I knew they must be worried about it getting back to their mothers. I really did think our explorations were over.

It was two days later, on a Saturday, that I discovered what having a reputation meant. Everybody was working on a strip right on the other side of the village. I had had to run an errand, and finished up walking alone to where they were. I went past the clocktower, to find it crowded with men in shabby uniforms leaning against the fence. They were Italian prisoners from the camp on the March road. You could see across the fields from Maltmas farm. As I passed they offered wooden snakes, painted green and marked with spots, that wriggled as they held them, rings and brooches made out of the glass from aeroplane windows. They made them in the evenings in the camps, after they had finished working in the fields, and tried to sell them in the village where they were allowed to walk about freely in their few hours off duty time. I often wondered why they did not escape back to Italy.

"Them Ities is lazy buggers," Uncle Jim had said when I asked him. "Too lazy be far to run away. Beside them know where they be well off. If they do get back 'ome, them 'll only 'ave to fight again, and them weren't all that keen on fighting in the first place."

They could be hired to work on the land, and when Jim had tried it he reckoned they were so lazy he did not get his money's worth. Later, the Italians moved out to be replaced by German prisoners, and he had a lot more respect for them:

"Them Jerries is like us," he said. "Them know what 'ard work is."

He had some working when he was pushed, and they worked so well he gave them a packet of Park Drive each to supplement the few pennies they got for their day's work. Sometimes they could play the village team at football and we would go and watch and have tea with them afterwards, of sardines and bread and jam.

That day, going past the Italians, I did think of buying a brooch for Dick, from the remains of my strawberry money, but I changed my mind because I thought she might think I was trying to bribe her or something. I dawdled along through the village to the country and out the other side, my thoughts full of Dick and the image of her laying in the straw. I was cursing the Millers now, especially since it did not seem to have got the girls into trouble.

I was just thinking of what I would like to do with Mad Miller's big front teeth, when I saw ahead a girl at the gate of a house to the left of the lane. As I got nearer, I could see she was slightly bigger than me, and that she was smiling.

"You're that evacuee boy from Maltmas, aren't you?" she said, still smiling.

I realised then where I had seen her before. Her name was Joyce and she was in a class one up from me at school.

"I 'eard about you," she said, and by the way she said it I knew what she had heard. She kept on talking, standing in front of me so that it was not easy to pass without pushing her out of the way.

It was a funny conversation, one sided, with her hardly stopping to breathe. Had I read in last Sunday's paper about the Germans keeping pretty women in a special camp and making them have it with S.S. Officers so that they reared a master race? She went on and on about it, and I got the impression she would have liked to have been one of the women at the camp.

Then, quite abruptly, she stopped, looked down at the ground and said:

"Would you like to see my map? My Mum and Dad are out working."

I could only think it was a funny thing to want to show anybody. Perhaps it was a Treasure map or something. I grinned and said:

"If yer want to . . ."

She took my hand and pulled me through the gate towards the red-bricked house.

"I knew you would," she said, "after I 'eard about you the other day."

When we got round to the back door she said:

"Nobody can see us 'ere. Ready?"

Suddenly she pulled down her knickers and hoisted her skirt. She stood proudly, watching my face for a reaction.

"That's my map," she said. "It's a good one, ain't it? Bet it's better than that Dick's or that Ida Davies . . ."

I could not take my eyes from it. There was not a bit of pink showing anywhere, it was so full of hair. I did not know what to say. I could only stare, first at her grinning face, and then down the thin white body.

Then I remembered that I was supposed to be with the others in the fields, and started to back away.

"I must be off. I'm supposed to be with Lou and Jim Bates . . ."

Her expression changed, the grin disappearing.

"Don't yer wan to see more?" she said. "There's a lot more I can show yer . . ."

But I was already running away up the path, and through the gate. When I had got up the road a bit, she reached the gate and yelled after me:

"Fuck off then. You'll never get another chance like that . . ."

It was funny. I did not want to explore with anyone else. Just Dick. When I got to the field, Aunt Lou asked me where I had been and why it had taken so long, but I could not tell her, of course.

A week later David and I came out after supper to find Dick, Ida and Dora in the lane. I knew then it was alright again, that the scare was over and we could start going out together again. I did not dare hope we could get as far as we had in the cowshed until we were walking around the edge of a meadow. I asked her what she wanted to do, and quite simply she said they wouldn't mind playing American airmen again.

There was a deep ditch by the field which was dry at that moment. We put our jackets down so that at least their bums would not get scratched. This time there were no Millers to interrupt and Dick and I lay together, exploring. David was not too sure that he wanted to, but he finally kept Dora amused. Ida just had to watch, waiting for her turn. I was excited and things happened to me below I had not experienced before.

But nothing could have been more innocent. The smiles, the kisses, the smell of the grass and rotting leaves, the comfort of each other together; they were all part of growing up. The pleasure was tinged with guilt then, and I would have been scared if I thought that Aunt Lou knew what we were doing, but I realised now that most people had similar first explorations with their own versions of Dick, Ida and Dora.

The exploration went on at other times, and my fingers learnt the contours of the female frame. Once it was in a shed right next to Dick's house, and her mother called her whilst we were together. I had to wait some time before appearing through the sack that covered the door so that the redness could have time to go from my face.

I think that Dick's mother knew. On one occasion Dick was wearing trousers and, deciding it would be easier in a dress, went into change while I waited outside. As she came out again her mother came to the door and said:

"Don't think I don't know why you want to change into a dress…"

She did not seem to say it in a serious tone, so we carried on. Often now Dick and I would go off together alone. At one stage, anyway, David had decided he did not want to do it any more. It became so open that I wonder why we were not caught in the act. Once it was on the side of a mound in a huge open field. People often used the path which ran alongside it to get to their smallholding, but fortunately nobody came. It has often occurred to me since that people may have passed by and we had not noticed so childishly engrossed were we in each other.

Dick was marvellous. She was as good at climbing trees and running and throwing as anybody, but she was very much a girl when she wanted to be. Once we got chased by the village policeman when we were scrumping in the Co-op orchard, and Dick was so fast that she was first out the other side on to the March road half a mile away.

We had grown into the life of Fridaybridge and Maltmas Farm. We learnt never to argue with Aunt Lou. Jim, Ron and Ludo had learnt ages ago, and always kept quiet if she was mad about something. At such times we learnt to stay out of her way by hiding in Flossie's huge kennel by the garden gate.

There were letters from home, generally addressed to Aunt Lou so that she could read the bits which referred to us. The doodlebugs had stopped. They were now getting some things called rockets which also did not have pilots, but which killed you before you knew what had hit you, Mum said.

Despite this danger, Aunt Lou's food, and even Dick, half of me still longed to be home. I think we both missed Mum and Dad badly, though neither of us said much about it.

Most of the time we were too busy to think. It was at night, laying in the big double bed, when the feeling crept into the stomach. During the day there was always something to do and forgetfulness came. Saturday was the best day of the week. Ron and Ludo would go off on the motorbike to King's Lynn, Peterborough or even Hunstanton. Sometimes we would go into Wisbech on the bus for the pictures, returning at tea-time for the whist drive and dance at the village hall.

There would always be a threepenny draw in between the two. Once, when Aunt Lou was not there, I won ten Woodbines. I smoked six of them before she got to hear about it the following Monday. When I won a half bottle of whisky, Aunt Lou took it away immediately, obviously convinced that I would have tottered home had she not.

We were allowed to stay to the dance, and I jigged around with Dick at one end. She invariably wore a pretty dress then, and I always wanted to get her outside, but she would never do anything then.

The band consisted of three fat men playing a piano, a trumpet and some drums. Saturday after Saturday they always played the same tunes but nobody seemed to mind.

They played on and on until late, at least eleven o'clock. Then we would all walk home together. The Donalds went down Maltmas Drive as well and Dick and I could hold hands without anybody noticing. It was as black as ink on the road, so dark that you could see every star there ever was, and there was hardly any part that was not smeared with a haze of white bodies.

On Sunday mornings the amusement was the village Home Guard, which met in the stackyard near Maltmas Farm. They

would do a very little shooting, bayonet practice or drill, with one eye
on their pocket watches for an emergency call to the Chequers the
moment it opened. The minute Uncle Jim finished his eggs, he
would put on his uniform and get out his gun from the wardrobe in
his bedroom. He was the smallest member of the platoon. Ludo said
he was their secret weapon because they could send him across a field
of normal height grass and the enemy would not notice until he stuck
a bayonet up their arses from below.

We used to sit on top of one of the haystacks and watch as they
tried to look serious and march between the houses of straw like a real
army. Always somebody fell over or turned the wrong way and spoilt
it, and we would laugh so much that they threw us out. The one
thing they were all good at was shooting. All of them had handled
guns before, and could bring down a moving bird or a rabbit easily.

"We'd never 'ave any trouble hitting a Jerry," Jim would say, but
I remember thinking, as I looked at his quarter-pint frame, that I
hoped he would never have to prove it.

The winter seemed to come quite suddenly. The ponds would get a
covering of ice, and as we went to school the grass would look like
cake icing. If there was a really deep frost Ron would go miles to
skate on one of the fenland dykes.

Chapter VII

It was on a cold Saturday night as we were going to the dance that we learnt that Aunt Lou was growing a bit tired of us. We had raced ahead out of Maltmas Farm and had hid a few yards up the road behind a hedge, ready to jump out on Lou and Jim. As they got nearer, we could hear Aunt Lou talking about Christmas.

"She needn't think I'm 'aving them bois for Christmas," she was saying. "She can come down and fetch them and they can come back at the turn of the year. It's a busy time, and I need a break from them . . ."

We jumped out then, but I had heard enough. I found it difficult to conceive that we were any trouble, or that Aunt Lou did not welcome us in the house at any time. In one way I was childishly disappointed to feel that Aunt Lou did not want us at any time, but in another way I was pleased. It meant that we might be going home, for a while anyway.

Aunt Lou must have written to Mum, because a few days before Christmas we went to meet Mum and Dad in Jim's car. I wanted to run forward and cuddle them both, but I thought that would be babyish and hung back. I'm sure they must have thought we liked it so much at Fridaybridge that we did not want to see them. Mum told all the neighbours that when we got home.

Aunt Lou had done a really special tea, with flan so topped with cream it looked like a small mountain in the middle of the table. Next day, after the usual huge Sunday dinner, Jim drove us all to the station. It was a long journey, and we had to change at Cambridge, but at last we were running through the black bricks of London, under a grey sky, past the smell of the Bow soap factory, into Liverpool Street Station.

On our way home Mum warned us about the rockets.

"As soon as the siren goes, get down into the shelter, dressed or not," she said. "They come so quickly there's 'ardly any warning."

As we turned the corner into John Fisher Street, I could see that Peabodys was as filthy, grimy, and lovely as ever. All around now there were gaping holes, or rough brick walls to fill up the gaps in terraces, but still K block was Peabodys' only casualty. We need not have gone away at all, I thought, but then I had visions of Dick in a green field and felt guilty and wondered if she was missing me.

We had again grown accustomed to going to sleep at night knowing that nothing was likely to disturb us until the morning except Uncle Jim's snoring from the next room. It came as a shock to be shaken, and to hear the wailing through a misty head and to be running down the stone stairs as if the legs did not belong.

Mum was right. We had no sooner sat down on a bunk in the shelter alongside the block than the explosions started. They were louder than anything I could remember before, and the double thick brick walls of the shelter seemed to come away from the cement that tried to clamp them together. I could see Mum was worried about us and wishing she had not agreed to have us home for Christmas.

But after the first couple of nights we got used to it again. Everybody else you met in the shelter and during the day seemed to have come to terms with it. They were just as cheerful, and there was just as much acceptance that if your number was on one of those rockets nothing could save you.

It certainly did not tone down the usual East End Christmas. There was singing and noise from almost every window and for days afterwards some of the people in the shelter were still drunk. We had Aunt Cissie and Uncle Ted up, and there were plenty of presents for us despite the rationing. Mum had saved her coupons and queued outside Freimullers, the Cable Street butchers, on Christmas Eve for hours to get the best.

It seemed no time at all before Mum was putting us on the train at Liverpool Street; and we were crawling out of the grime past the soap factory again. I wished then we had not gone home. It had made me realise that London was still the only real place in the world and I was so homesick I felt like pulling the communication cord and getting out. I could see from the look on David's face that he felt much the same way. That night, in the big double bed, I allowed myself to cry for the first time in ages, but I did not do it so that anybody could hear.

It was great to see Dick again, and to realise that she really had missed me. Almost at once, though I started to get huge boils at the back of my neck which made Aunt Lou say I was so vain I was trying to grow two heads.

They got bigger and bigger and would not go away. When Aunt Lou wrote home about them, Mum said in her letter that it was because of the shock of the rockets. I could not see this at all: David did not even get a pimple on his bum and he had felt just as many rockets coming down. The boils were not too bad. It was Aunt Lou's way of treating them that really hurt.

"You 'as to get out the core, then it'll be all right," she would say.

She would sit me on a chair facing the wrong way. Then she would give me a towel to bite into as she squeezed and squeezed at the molehills on my neck. When she got a core out she would show it to me among the mixture of white and bloody mess on the cloth she was using. For all the squeezing and for all the cores it seemed to be months before the crop stopped growing.

I was violently homesick for what seemed a long time. The village dance did not seem so exciting, and even the Sunday morning soldiers did not look so funny. I think Aunt Lou was pleased to see us back, though overhearing the conversation that night before Christmas had made me uncertain even about that. It was too cold to be with Dick outside four brick walls, and there was not even that to relieve the boredom.

A few weeks after we returned something happened which added to the winter darkness and the depression. Old Sam Hooker hanged himself in the stakes at Maltmas Farm. Jim found him one morning. He had been hanging there all night, and it gave me the willies to think that we had been sleeping only a few yards away as he swung to and fro by his wrinkled neck. It had all been quite deliberate, Uncle Jim said later, unnecessarily. He had obviously brought in his horse, fed and watered him and bedded him down for the night. Then he had thrown a rope from the beam and choked to death as the horse munched his feed.

The village policemen came down and we saw them collect Sam Hooker in a van. It was the talk of Fridaybridge for weeks afterwards. Sam Hooker was only about sixty, though everybody called him Old. He had always seemed cheerful enough as he put his horse away at nights. His missus had died two years previously and he lived all alone, not even calling in at the Chequers.

"Expect he got fed up with his own company," said Aunt Lou when they were still talking about it weeks later.

Right from the day Jim found him I would always run past the stables at night. It seemed right that there should be some sort of ghost after he had hung there for so long.

The country was quiet, and there was nothing to watch in the fields. Jim, Ron and Ludo spent most of their time repairing the buildings and the farming things. It was all so boring, with the swinging oil lamp in the kitchen lit before we got home from school, and hardly being allowed out at all in the dark.

Then, suddenly, life came back again. One morning, on the way to school, I noticed a field with a five o'clock shadow of spring wheat on its brown face. The birds seemed to have come back, and the Bates family were busy in the fields again. The evenings took in some light, and I could meet Dick outside schooltime again. But we could not get back to the intimacy we had enjoyed. We still liked each other, but we did not spring together automatically into our ways of the last summer and autumn. Perhaps the time for exploration had passed, and there was no way we could go further because of our age.

Dad's letters from home were more cheerful. The rockets seemed to be getting fewer and fewer. He said he thought that, at last, the Führer was running out of ready cash.

I wished he would also say it was safe for us to come home, especially since we had fallen out with Ron and Ludo.

It started when they found the baby sparrows in the barn, their eyes not yet open, and their mouths open for food at the slightest sound. We met them coming across the yard holding the nest with the birds still in it.

"They're lovely," said David.

"Them's pests," said Ron.

"They eats all the crops," added Ludo.

"Wot yer gonna do with 'em then?"

"Only one thing with sparrows – drown 'em," said Ron.

We shouted at him, calling him a bloody murderer, but it did not stop him. He pushed the nest deep down into the water barrel which caught the rain from the barn roof. After two or three minutes he scooped out the little shapes and fed them to the cats that lived half in the barn and half on Lou's house porch.

"The ways of the country is 'ard, boi," he said to me when he saw the way I was looking at him. "Can't afford to 'ave them eating good crops at the best o' times, let alone when there's a war on."

My final disenchantment with Fridaybridge, and Ludo especially, came one Sunday afternoon when we had nothing to do. Ludo and some older boys had condescended to walk with us over the fields behind the house. We met Dick, out on her own, near her house. She was the only girl amongst six boys.

At first it was a game. All the boys chased Dick. She laughed and seemed to like it, and I was jealous. Then it all went nasty. Somebody had brought her down in the grass beneath a tree, and somebody else had said:

"Let's 'ave 'er trousers off . . ."

And though she struggled, they did. As Ludo played with her, Dick was crying, and I let him, without trying to defend her, without even a word. When they let her up she ran away, pulling up her trousers. I felt sick. I could never really look Dick in the eye again. I saw her at school, but she never came down to Maltmas in the evenings, and I was too ashamed to go to her.

Fortunately, I did not have to face her for long. A letter from Dad said that he and Mum thought it was safe for us to return to London. I wondered how long it would be safe for this time, and what other flying weapon Hitler would produce to make us go away again.

I don't believe I even said goodbye to Dick. David and I were both pleased to be going home as we were put onto the train in Wisbech. I thought there was a brightness about Aunt Lou's eyes I had not seen before. It might even have been caused by tears.

"We'll miss you bois," she said as the train began to move.

I knew we would miss the Yorkshire puddings, the cream and the butter.

Chapter VIII

After we returned the siren never went again. We were always ready. Ma put out the spare blankets and made a flask of hot sweet tea every night – just in case. The shelter got dusty and smelly with misuse. Drunks began to pee in the doorways, the bunks were used to jump up and down on.

Nobody could really believe, though, that Hitler would really leave us alone.

"He's probably too busy inventing something new to send any bombers – but something is bound to 'appen soon," said Mum.

I kept thinking that if he did we would have to go away again, and dreaded it.

But nothing ever did. At the school we were now going to in Fairclough Street, our new Jewish schoolmaster would have flags each day on a map of Europe to show us where our troops were that morning. As the British and American flags got nearer the Russian ones, he said he could confidently state we were winning.

Then, one day, the world around Peabodys went mad. The ships in the docks sounded their sirens. The kids lit a bonfire in the street, which got so hot it cracked the cobbles, and the effigies of Hitler, Goebbels and Goering lasted only a few seconds before they were consumed.

Hitler was dead and the Germans had surrendered. A few weeks later we had something called a VE-Day. The Peabody's organised a big party. The square was full of wooden tables borrowed from St Paul's and, although the rationing was still on, everybody made cakes from something they had stacked away for a day such as this.

There was a big parade and we queued for hours and hours to see rank after rank of soldiers going past for hour after hour. I wondered what they were doing there when everybody kept saying that we must not talk too soon because we still had the Japs to beat.

As it turned out, we had no need to worry about the Yellow Peril, as Dad called them. It did not seem five minutes before the papers were blaring that Japan had surrendered. The Americans had had to drop only two bombs on them before they folded up. They obviously could not take a whole blitz like us Londoners, I thought.

Then we collected wood from the bomb sites for a VJ night fire. The pile got bigger and bigger up the side of B block, and each day they had to raise the effigy of Tojo a little higher so that he still sat on top.

After we had all sung and done knees-ups as Tojo burned, Mum said:

"Well, it really is over now."

I realised that David and I were now home in Peabody's for good, and that there really would be no more 'rotten places, far, far away'.